William Stanley Jevons

Political Economy

William Stanley Jevons

Political Economy

ISBN/EAN: 9783337073671

Printed in Europe, USA, Canada, Australia, Japan

Cover: Foto ©Suzi / pixelio.de

More available books at **www.hansebooks.com**

Science Primers.

·POLITICAL

ECONOMY.·

BY

W. STANLEY JEVONS, LL.D., M.A., F.R.S.,

PROFESSOR OF POLITICAL ECONOMY IN UNIVERSITY COLLEGE, LONDON;
EXAMINER IN LOGIC AND MORAL PHILOSOPHY IN THE
UNIVERSITY OF LONDON.

NEW YORK:

D. APPLETON AND COMPANY,

549 AND 551 BROADWAY.

1880.

CONTENTS.

PREFACE.

In preparing this little treatise, I have tried to put the truths of Political Economy into a form suitable for elementary instruction. While connected with Owens College, it was my duty, as Cobden Lecturer on Political Economy, to instruct a class of pupil-teachers, in order that they might afterwards introduce the teaching of this important subject into elementary schools. There can be no doubt that it is most desirable to disseminate knowledge of the truths of political economy through all classes of the population by any means which may be available. From ignorance of these truths arise many of the worst social evils—disastrous strikes and lockouts, opposition to improvements, improvidence, destitution, misguided charity, and discouraging failure in many well-intended measures. More than forty years ago Miss Martineau successfully popularised the truths of political economy in her admirable tales. About the same time, Archbishop Whately was much struck with the need of inculcating knowledge of these matters at an early age. With this view he prepared his " Easy Lessons on Money Matters," of which many editions have been printed. In early boyhood I learned my first ideas of political economy from a copy of these lessons, from the preface to which I quote these remarks of Whately : " The rudiments of sound knowledge concerning these (subjects) may, it has been found by experience, be communicated at a very early age. . . . Those, therefore, who are engaged in conducting, or in patronising or promoting education, should consider it a matter of no small moment to instil, betimes, just notions on subjects with which all must in after-life be practically conversant, and in which no class of men, from the highest to the lowest, can, in such a country as this at least, be safely left in ignorance or in error." In later years like opinions have been held and efforts made by Mr. William Ellis, Professor W. B. Hodgson, Dr. John Watts, Mr. Templar, and others, and experience seems to confirm both the need and the practicability of the teaching advocated by Whately. But it is evident that one condition of success in such efforts is the possession of a small text-book exactly suited to the purposes in view. Relying upon my experience of ten years in the instruction of pupil-teachers at Manchester, I have now put my lessons into the simplest form which the nature of the subject seems to render advisable.

It is hoped that this little treatise may also serve as a stepping-stone to a knowledge of the science among general readers of maturer age, who have hitherto neglected the study of political economy.

Owing to the narrow limits of the space at my disposal, it was impossible to treat the whole of the science in a satisfactory way. I have, therefore, omitted some parts of political economy altogether, and have passed over other parts very briefly. Thus the larger portion of my space has been reserved for such subjects as Production, Division of Labour, Capital and Labour, Trades-Unions, and Commercial Crises, which are most likely to be interesting and useful to readers of this Primer.

UNIVERSITY COLLEGE,
GOWER STREET, LONDON, W.C.
31st January, 1878.

POLITICAL ECONOMY.

CHAPTER I.—INTRODUCTION.

1. **What is Political Economy?** Political Economy treats of **the wealth of nations**; it inquires into the causes which make one nation more rich and prosperous than another. It aims at teaching what should be done in order that poor people may be as few as possible, and that everybody may, as a general rule, be well paid for his work. Other sciences, no doubt, assist us in reaching the same end. The science of mechanics shows how to obtain force, and how to use it in working machines. Chemistry teaches how useful substances may be produced—how beautiful dyes and odours and oils, for instance, may be extracted from the disagreeable refuse of the gas-works. Astronomy is necessary for the navigation of the oceans. Geology guides in the search for coal and metals.

Various social sciences, also, are needed to promote the welfare of mankind. Jurisprudence treats of the legal rights of persons, and how they may be best defined and secured by just laws. Political Philosophy inquires into the different forms of government and their relative advantages. Sanitary Science ascertains the causes of disease. The science of Statistics collects all manner of facts relating to the state or community. All these sciences are useful in showing how we may be made more healthy, wealthy, and wise.

But **Political Economy** is distinct from all these other sciences, and treats of **wealth** itself; it inquires what wealth is; how we can best consume it when we have got it; and how we may take advantage of the other sciences to get it. People are fond of finding fault with political economy, because **it treats only of wealth**; they say that there are many better things than wealth, such as virtue, affection, generosity. They would have us study these good qualities rather than mere wealth. A man may grow rich by making hard bargains, and saving up his money like a miser. Now as this is not nearly so good as if he were to spend his wealth for the benefit of his relatives, friends, and the public generally, they proceed to condemn the science of wealth.

But these complainers misunderstand the purpose of a science like political economy. They do not see that in learning we must do one thing at a time. We cannot learn the social sciences all at the same time. No one objects to astronomy that it treats only of the stars, or to mathematics that it treats only of numbers and quantities. It would be a very curious Science Primer which should treat of astronomy, geology, chemistry, physics, physiology, &c., all at once. There must be many physical sciences, and there must be also many social sciences, and each of these sciences must treat of its own proper subject, and not of things in general.

2. **Mistakes about Political Economy.** A great many mistakes are made about the science we are going to consider by people who ought to know better. These mistakes often arise from people thinking that they understand all about political economy without studying it. No ordinary person of sense ventures to contradict a chemist about chemistry, or an astronomer about eclipses, or even a geologist about rocks and fossils. But everybody has his opinion one way or another about bad trade, or the effect of high wages, or the harm of being underbid by cheap labour, or any one of hundreds of questions of social importance. It does not occur to such people that these matters are really more difficult to understand than chemistry, or astronomy, or geology, and that a lifetime of study is not sufficient to enable

us to speak confidently about them. Yet, they who have never studied political economy at all, are usually the most confident.

The fact is that, just as physical science was formerly hated, so now there is a kind of ignorant dislike and impatience of political economy. People wish to follow their own impulses and prejudices, and are vexed when told that they are doing just what will have the opposite effect to that which they intend. Take the case of **so-called charity**. There are many good-hearted people who think that it is virtuous to give alms to poor people who ask for them, without considering the effect produced upon the people. They see the pleasure of the beggar on getting the alms, but they do not see the after effects, namely, that beggars become more numerous than before. Much of the poverty and crime which now exist have been caused by mistaken charity in past times, which has caused a large part of the population to grow up careless, and improvident, and idle. Political economy proves that, instead of giving casual ill-considered alms, we should educate people, teach them to work and earn their own livings, and save up something to live upon in old age. If they continue idle and improvident, they must suffer the results of it. But as this seems hard-hearted treatment, political economists are condemned by soft-hearted and mistaken people. The science is said to be a dismal, cold-blooded one, and it is implied that the object of the science is to make the rich richer, and to leave the poor to perish. All this is quite mistaken.

The political economist, when he inquires how people may most easily acquire riches, does not teach that the rich man should keep his wealth like a miser, nor spend it in luxurious living like a spendthrift. There is absolutely nothing in the science to dissuade the rich man from spending his wealth generously and yet wisely. He may prudently help his relatives and friends ; he may establish useful public institutions, such as free public libraries, museums, public parks, dispensaries, &c. ; he may assist in educating the poor, or promoting institutions for higher education ; he may relieve any who are suffering from misfortunes which could not have been provided against ; cripples, blind people, and all who are absolutely disabled from helping themselves, are proper objects of the rich man's charity.   All that the political economist insists upon is that **charity shall be really charity, and shall not injure those whom it is intended to aid.**   It is sad to think that hitherto much harm has been done by those who wished only to do good.

It is sad, again, to see thousands of persons trying to improve their positions by means which have just the opposite effect, I mean by strikes, by refusing to use machinery, and by trying, in various ways, to resist the production of wealth.   Working men have made a political economy of their own: they want to make themselves rich by taking care not to produce too much riches.   They, again, see an immediate effect of what they do, but they do not see what happens as the after result.   It is the same with the question of Free Trade.   In England we have at length learned the wisdom of leaving commerce free.   In other countries, and even in the Australian Colonies, laws are yet passed to make people richer by preventing them from using the abundant products of other lands.   People actually refuse to see that wealth must be increased by producing it where it can be produced most easily and plentifully.   Each trade, each town, each nation must furnish what it can yield most cheaply, and other goods must be bought from the places where they also can be raised most easily.

Political economy teaches us to look beyond the immediate effect of what we do, and to seek the good of the whole community, and even of the whole of mankind.   The present prosperity of England is greatly due to the science which Adam Smith gave to the world in his "Wealth of Nations."   He taught us the value of **Free Labour and Free Trade,** and now, a hundred years after the publication of his great book, there ought not to be so many mistaken people vainly acting in opposition to his lessons. It is certain that **if people do not understand a true political economy, they will make a false one of their own.** Hence the imperative need that no one, neither man nor woman, should grow up without acquiring some comprehension of the science which we are going to study.

3. **Divisions of the Science.** I will begin by stating the order in which the several branches or divisions of the science of economy are to be considered in this little treatise. Firstly, we must learn what wealth, the subject of the science, consists of. Secondly, we proceed to inquire how wealth is used or consumed; nothing, we shall see, can be wealth, unless it be put to some use, and before we make wealth we must know what we want to use. Thirdly, we can go on to consider how wealth is produced or brought into existence; and how, in the fourth place, having been produced, it is shared among the different classes of people who have had a hand in producing it. Briefly, we may say that political economy treats of (1) **The Nature,** (2) **The Consumption,** (3) **The Production,** and (4) **The Distribution of Wealth.** It will also be necessary to say a little about **Taxation.** A part of the wealth of every country must be taken by the government, in order to pay the expenses of defending and governing the nation. But taxation may come, perhaps, under the head of distribution.

4. **Wealth and Natural Riches.** We do not learn anything by reading that **political economy is the science of wealth,** unless we know what science is, and what wealth is. When one term is defined by means of other terms, we must understand these other terms, in order to get any light upon the subject. In the Primer of Logic I have already

attempted to explain what science is, and I will now attempt to make plain what wealth is.

Doubtless many people think that there is no difficulty in knowing what **wealth** is; the real difficulty is to get it. But in this they are mistaken. There are a great many people in this country who have made themselves rich, and few or none of them would be able to explain clearly what wealth is. In fact it is not at all easy to decide the question. The popular idea is that wealth consists of money, and money consists of gold and silver; the wealthy man, then, would be one who has an iron safe full of bags of gold and silver money. But this is far from being the case; rich men, as a general rule, have very little money in their possession. Instead of bags of money they keep good balances at their bankers. But this again does not tell us what wealth is, because it is difficult to say what a bank balance consists of; the balance is shown by a few figures in the bankers' books. As a general rule the banker has not got in his possession the money which he owes to his customers.

Perhaps some one will say that he is beyond question rich, who owns a great deal of land. But this depends entirely upon where and what the land is. A man who owns an English county is very wealthy; a man might own an equal extent of land in Australia, without being remarkably rich. The savages of Australia, who held the land before the English took it, had enormous quantities of land, but they were nevertheless miserably poor. Thus it is plain that land alone is not wealth.

It may be urged that, in order to form wealth, the land should be fertile, the soil should be good, the rivers and lakes abounding in fish, and the forests full of good timber. Under the ground there should be plenty of coal, iron, copper, reefs of gold, &c. If, in addition to these, there is a good climate, plenty of sunlight, and enough, but not too much, water, then the country is certainly **rich.** It is true that these things have been called **natural riches;** but I mention them in order to point out that they are not in themselves wealth. People may live upon land full of natural riches, as the North American Indians lived upon the country which now forms the United States; nevertheless they may be very poor, because they cannot, or they will not labour, in such a way as **to turn the natural riches into wealth.**✓ On the other hand, people like the Dutch live upon very poor bits of land, and yet become wealthy by skill, industry and providence. The fact is that wealth is more due to labour and ingenuity than to a good soil or climate ; but all these things are needed in order that people shall become as rich as the inhabitants of England, France, the United States, or Australia.

5. **What is Wealth ?** Nassau Senior, one of the best writers on political economy, defined **wealth** in these words : **Under that term we comprehend all those things, and those things only, which are transferable, are limited in supply, and are directly or indirectly productive of pleasure, or preventive of pain.** It is necessary to understand, in the first place, exactly what Senior meant. According to him, whatever is comprehended under wealth must have three distinct qualities, and whatever has these three qualities must be a part of wealth. If these qualities are rightly chosen, we get a correct definition, which, as explained in the *Logic Primer* (section 44), is a precise statement of the qualities which are just sufficient to make out a class, and to tell us what things belong to it and what do not. Instead, however, of the long phrase " directly or indirectly productive of pleasure or preventive of pain," we may substitute the single word **useful,** and we may then state the definition in this simple way :—

Wealth $=$ **what is** $\begin{cases} \text{(1) transferable.} \\ \text{(2) limited in supply.} \\ \text{(3) useful.} \end{cases}$

We still need to learn exactly what is meant by the three qualities of wealth; we must learn what it is to be transferable, limited in supply, and useful.

6. **Wealth is transferable.** By being **transferable,** we mean that a thing can be passed over (Latin, *trans*, across, and *fero*, I carry) from one person to another. Sometimes things can be literally handed over, like a watch or a book; sometimes they can be transferred by a written deed, or by legal possession, as in the case of land and houses; services, also, can be transferred, as when a footman hires himself to a master. Even a musician or a preacher transfers his services, when his auditors have the benefit of hearing him. But there are many desirable things which cannot be transferred from one person to another; a rich man can hire a footman, but he cannot buy the footman's good health; he can hire the services of the best physician, but if these services fail to restore health, there is no help. So, too, it is impossible really to buy or sell the love of relatives, the esteem of friends, the happiness of a good conscience. Wealth may do a great deal, but it cannot really ensure those things which are more precious than pearls and rubies. Political economy does not pretend to examine all the causes of happiness, and those moral riches which cannot be bought and sold are no part of wealth in our present use of the word. The poor man who has a good conscience, affectionate friends, and good health, may really be much happier than the rich man, who is deprived of such blessings; but, on the other hand, a man need not lose his good conscience, and his other sources of happiness when he becomes rich and enjoys all the interesting occupations and amusements which wealth can give. **Wealth, then, is far from being the only good thing: nevertheless it is good,** because it saves us from too severe labour, from the fear of actual want, and enables us to buy such pleasant things and services as are transferable.

7. **Wealth is limited in Supply.** In the second place, things cannot be called wealth unless they be **limited in supply**; if we have just as much of any substance as we want, then we shall not esteem a new supply of it. Thus the air around us is not wealth in ordinary circumstances, because we have only to open our mouths and we get as much as we can use. What air we do actually breathe is exceedingly useful, because it keeps us alive; but we usually pay nothing for it, because there is plenty for all. In a diving bell, or a deep mine, however, air becomes limited in supply, and then may be considered a part of wealth. When the tunnel under the English Channel is completed, it will be a great question how to get air to breathe in the middle of it. Even in the Metropolitan Railway tunnel a little more fresh air would be very valuable.

On the other hand diamonds, though much valued, are used for few purposes; they make beautiful ornaments and they serve to cut glass or to bore rocks. Their high value chiefly arises from the fact that they are scarce. Of course scarcity alone will not create value. There are many scarce metals, or minerals, of which only a few little bits have ever yet been seen; but such substances are not valuable, unless some special use has been found for them. The metal iridium is sold at a very high price because it is wanted for making the tips of gold pens, and can be got only in small quantities.

8. **Wealth is useful.** In the third place, we can easily see that everything which forms a part of wealth must be **useful**, or have **utility**, that is, it must serve some purpose, or be agreeable and desirable in some way or other. Senior said correctly that **useful things are those which directly or indirectly produce pleasure or prevent pain.** A well tuned and well played musical instrument produces pleasure; a dose of medicine prevents pain to one who is in need of it. But it is often impossible to decide

whether things give more pleasure or prevent more pain; dinner saves us from the pain of hunger and gives us the pleasure of eating good things. There is utility so far as pleasure is increased and pain decreased; nor does it matter, as far as political economy is concerned, what is the nature of the pleasure.

Then, again, we need not be particular as to whether things **directly produce pleasure,** like the clothes we wear, or whether they **indirectly** do so, as in the cases of the machines employed to make the clothes. Things are indirectly useful when, like tools, machines, materials, &c., they are only wanted to make other things, which shall be actually consumed and enjoyed by some person. The carriage in which a person takes a pleasant drive is directly useful; the baker's cart which brings him food is indirectly useful. But sometimes we can hardly distinguish. Shall we say that the meat put into the mouth is directly, but the fork which puts it in is indirectly, useful?

9. **Commodity.** We now know exactly what is wealth; but instead of speaking continually of wealth, it will often be convenient to speak of commodities, or goods. **A commodity is any portion of wealth**—anything, therefore, which is useful, and transferable, and limited in supply. Wool, cotton, iron, tea, books, boots, pianos, &c., are all commodities in certain circumstances, but not in all circumstances. Wool on a stray sheep lost in the mountains is not a commodity, nor iron in a mine which cannot be worked. **A commodity, in short, is anything which is really useful and wanted, so that people will buy or sell it.** But, instead of the long word commodity, I shall often use the shorter word goods, and the reader should remember that

goods = commodities = portion of wealth.

CHAPTER II.

UTILITY.

10. **Our Wants are various.** After a little reflection, we shall see that we generally want but little of any one kind of commodity, and prefer to have a portion of one kind and a portion of another kind. Nobody likes to make his dinner off potatoes only, or bread only, or even beef only; he prefers to have some beef, some bread, some potatoes, besides, perhaps, beer, pudding, &c. Similarly, a man would not care to have many suits of clothes all alike; he may wish to have several suits, no doubt, but then some should be warmer, others thinner; some for evening dress, others for travelling, and so on. A library all made of copies of the same book would be absurd; to keep several exact duplicates of any work would be generally useless. A collector of engravings would not care to have many identical copies of the same engraving. In all these, and many other cases, we learn that **human wants tend towards variety; each separate want is soon satis-fied, or made full** (Latin, *satis*, enough, and *facere*, to make), and then some other want begins to be felt. This was called by Senior **the law of variety**, and it is the most important law in the whole of political economy.

It is easy to see, too, that there is a natural order in which our wants follow each other as regards importance; we must have food to eat, and if we cannot get anything else we are glad to get bread; next we want meat, vegetables, fruit, and other delicacies. Clothing is not on the whole as necessary as food; but, when a man has plenty to eat, he begins to think of dressing himself well. Next comes the question of a house to live in; a mere cabin is better than nothing, but the richer a man is the larger the house he likes to have.   When he has got a good house he wants to fill it with furniture, books, pictures, musical instruments, articles of vertu, and so forth.   Thus we can lay down very roughly **a law of succession of wants,** somewhat in this order : air, food, clothing, lodging, literature, articles of adornment and amusement.

It is very important to observe that there is no end nor limit to the number of various things which a rich man will like to have, if he can get them.   He who has got one good house begins to wish for another : he likes to have one house in town, another in the country.   Some dukes and other very rich people have four, five, or more houses.   From these observations we learn that there can never be, among civilised nations, so   much   wealth,   that   people would cease to wish for any more.   However much we manage to produce, there are still many other things which we want to acquire.   When people are well fed, they begin to want good clothing; when they are well clothed, they want good houses, and furniture, and objects of art.   If, then, too much wealth were ever produced, it would be **too much of   one   sort,   not   too   much   of   all   sorts.** Farmers might be ruined if they grew so much corn that nobody could eat it all; then, instead of producing so much corn, they ought to produce more beef and milk.   Thus there is no fear that, by machinery or other improvements, things will be made so plentifully that workmen would be thrown out of employment, and not wanted any more.   If men were not required at one trade, they would only need to learn a new trade.

11. **When things are useful.**   The chief question to consider, then, is when things are useful and when they are not.   **This entirely depends upon whether we want them or not.**   Most things about us, the air, rain water, stones, soil, &c., are not wealth, because we do not want them, or want so little

that we can readily get what we need. Let us consider carefully whether we can say that **water is useful,** or in what sense we may say so. It is common to hear people say that water is the most useful substance in the world, and so it is—in the right place, and at the right time. But if water is too plentiful and flows into your cellars, it is not useful there; if it soaks through the walls and produces rheumatism, it is hurtful, not useful. If a man wanting pure good water, digs a well and the water comes, it is useful. But if, in digging a coal pit, water rushes in and prevents the miners reaching the coal seam, it is clear that the water is the opposite of useful. In some countries rain comes very irregularly and uncertainly. In Australia the droughts last for one or two or even three years, and in the interior of the continent the rivers sometimes dry up altogether. The dirtiest pools then become very valuable· for keeping the flocks of sheep alive. In New South Wales water has been sold for three shillings a bucketful. When a drought breaks up, sudden floods come down the rivers, destroying the dams and bridges, sweeping away houses, and often drowning men and animals. It is quite plain that we cannot say water is always useful; it is often so hurtful as to ruin and drown people. All that we can really say is that **water is useful when and where we want it, and** **in such quantity as we want, and not otherwise.** We must not say that all water is useful, but only that such water is useful as we can actually use.

It is now easy to see why things, in order to be wealth, must be **limited in supply**; for we never want an unlimited quantity of anything. A man cannot drink more than two or three quarts of water in the day, nor eat more than a few pounds of food. Thus we can understand why in South America, where there are great herds of cattle, the best beef is not wealth, namely, because there is so much that there are not people enough to eat it. The beef which is eaten there is just as useful in nourishing people as beef eaten in England, but it is not so valuable because there is plenty of beef to spare, that is, plenty of beef not wanted by the people.

12. **What we must aim at.** Now we can see precisely what it is that we have to learn in political economy. It is **how to supply our various wants as fully as possible.** To do this we must, first of all, ascertain what things are wanted. There is no use making things unless, when made, they are useful, and the quantities of things must be proportioned to what are wanted. The cabinetmaker must not make a great many tables, and few chairs; he must make some tables and more chairs. Similarly, every kind of commodity must be supplied when it is most wanted; and nothing must be over-supplied, that is manufactured in such large quantities that it would have been better to spend the labour in manufacturing other things.

Secondly, we must always try to produce things with the least possible labour; for labour is painful exertion, and we wish to undergo as little pain and trouble as we can. Thus, as Professor Hearn, of the University of Melbourne, well described it, **political economy is the science of efforts to satisfy wants**; it teaches us how to find the shortest way to what we wish for. The object which we aim at is **to obtain the most riches at the cost of the least labour.**

13. **When to consume wealth.** To consume a commodity is to destroy its utility, as when coal is burnt, or bread eaten, or a jug broken, or a piano worn out. Things lose their utility in various ways, as when they go bad, like meat and fish; when the fashion changes, as with ladies' attire; or when they merely grow old, as in the case of an almanack, or a directory. Again, houses fall into bad repair; ricks of corn may be burnt down; ships may founder. In

all these cases utility is destroyed, slowly or quickly, and the commodities may be said to be consumed. It is obvious that we must use things while they are fit to be used, if we are to use them at all.

It is evident, too, that we ought to try to get the utmost possible use out of things which we are happy enough to possess. If an object is not injured nor destroyed by use, as in the case of reading a book, or looking at a picture, then the more often we use it the greater is the utility. Such things become more useful if they are passed on from one person to another, like books in a circulating library. In this case there arises what we may call **the multiplication of utility.** Public libraries, museums, picture galleries and like institutions all multiply utility, and the cost of such institutions is little or nothing compared with their usefulness.

When a commodity is destroyed at once by use, as in the case of food, it is obvious that only one person can use the same portion of commodity. Our object must then be to consume it when it is most useful. If a man lost in the bush find himself with a short supply of food, it would be foolish of him to eat it all up at once, when he might starve for several days afterwards. He should spread out his supply, so as to eat each bit of food when it will support his strength the most. So we ought to do with the earnings of a life time. The working man should not spend all his wages when trade is brisk, because he will want some of it much more when trade becomes slack, and he is out of employment. Similarly, that which is spent in early life upon mere luxuries and frivolities, might be much more useful in old age, when even necessaries and ordinary comforts may be difficult to obtain. **All wealth is produced in order that it may be consumed, but then it must be consumed when it best fulfils its purpose; that is, when it is most useful.**

14. **The Fallacy of Consumption.** It is not

uncommon to hear people say that they ought to spend money freely in order to encourage trade. If every person were to save his money instead of spending it, trade, they think, would languish and workmen would be out of employment. Tradespeople favour these notions, because it is obvious that, the more a milliner or draper can persuade his customer to buy, the more profit he makes thereby. The customers, too, are quite inclined to think the argument a good one, because they enjoy buying new dresses, and other pleasant things. Nevertheless **the argument is a bad fallacy.**

The fact is, that a person who has riches cannot help employing labour of some kind or other. If he saves up his money he probably puts it into a bank; but the banker does not keep it idle. The banker lends it out again to merchants, manufacturers and builders, who use it to increase their business and employ more hands. If he buy railway shares or government funds, those who receive the money put it to some other profitable use. If the rich man actually hoards up his money in the form of gold or silver, he gets no advantage from it, but he creates so much more demand for gold or silver. If many rich people were to take to hoarding up gold, the result would be to make gold mining more profitable, and there would be so many more gold miners, instead of railway navvies, or other workmen.

We see then that, when a rich person decides how to spend his money he is deciding not how many more workpeople shall be set to work, but what kind of work they shall do. If he decide to give a grand fancy ball, then in the end there will be so many more milliners, costumiers, lacemakers, confectioners, &c. A single ball indeed will have no great effect; but, if many people were to do the same, there would soon be more tradespeople attracted to these trades. If, on the other hand, rich people invest their money in a new railway, there will be so many more surveyors, engineers, foremen, navvies, iron puddlers, iron rollers, engine mechanics, carriage builders, &c.

The question really comes to this, whether people are made happier by more fancy balls, or by more railways. A fancy ball creates amusement at the time, but it costs a great deal of money, especially to the guests who buy expensive costumes. When it is over there is no permanent result, and no one is much the better for it. The railway, on the other hand, is no immediate cause of pleasure, but it cheapens goods by enabling them to be carried more easily : it allows people to live in the country, instead of the crowded town, or it carries them on pleasant and wholesome excursions.

We see, then, that it is simple folly to approve of consumption for its own sake, or because it benefits trade. In spending our wealth we ought to think solely of the advantage which people get out of that spending.

15. **The Fallacy of Non-consumption.** Some people fall into the opposite fallacy of thinking that all spending is an evil. The best thing to do with wealth is to keep it and let it grow by interest, or even to neglect the interest and keep the gold itself. Thus they become what we call misers, and there are always a certain number of people, who deprive themselves of the ordinary pleasures of life, in order that they may have the pleasure of feeling rich. Now these kind of people do no positive harm to their fellow-men ; on the contrary they increase the wealth of the country, and some one or other will sooner or later benefit by it. Moreover, if they put their wealth into banks and other good investments, they do great service in increasing the capital of the nation, and thus enabling so many more factories, docks, railways, and other important works to be constructed. Most people are so fond of spending their money on passing amusements, entertainments, eating and drinking, and fine dressing, that it is a distinct advantage to have other

people who will put their wealth into a more permanently useful form.

Nevertheless, there could be no use in abstaining from all enjoyment in order that we might lay up a store of wealth. Things are not wealth unless they are useful and pleasant to us. If everybody invested his savings in railway shares, we should have so many railways that they could not be all used, and they would become rather a nuisance than a benefit. Similarly, there could be no good in building docks unless there were ships to load in them, nor ships unless there were goods or passengers to convey. It would be equally absurd to make cotton mills if there were already enough to manufacture as much cotton goods as people could consume.

Thus we come to see that wealth must be fitted for use and consumption in some way or other. What we have to do is to endeavour to spend our means so as to get the greatest real happiness for ourselves, our relatives, friends, and all other people whom we ought to consider.

CHAPTER III.

PRODUCTION OF WEALTH.

16. The **Requisites of Production.** The first thing in industry, as we now see, is to decide what we want; the next thing is to get it, or make it, or, as we shall say, **produce it,** and we ought obviously to produce it with the least possible labour. To learn how this may be done, we must inquire what is needful for the production of wealth. There are, as is commonly and correctly said, **three requisites of production**; before we can, in the present state of society, undertake to produce wealth, we must have the three following things :—

(1) **Land,**
(2) **Labour,**
(3) **Capital.**

In production we bring these things together; we apply labour to the land, and we employ the capital in assisting the labourer with tools, and feeding him while he is engaged on the work. We must now proceed to consider each of the three requisites in succession.

17. Land or Source of Materials. The word **production** is a very good one; it means **drawing forth** (Latin, *pro*, before, and *ducere*, to draw), and it thus exactly expresses the fact that, when we want to create wealth, we have to go to some piece of land, or to some lake, river, or sea, and draw forth the substance which is to be made into wealth. It does not matter whether the material comes from the surface of the earth, or from mines and quarries sunk into the earth, or from seas and oceans. Our food mostly grows upon the land, as in the case of corn, potatoes, cattle, game, &c.; our clothes are chiefly made of cotton, flax, wool, skins, raised in like manner. Minerals and metals are obtained by sinking pits and mines into the crust of the earth. Rivers, lakes, seas, and oceans are no slight source of wealth : they yield food, oil, whalebone, sealskin, &c. We cannot manufacture any goods unless we have some matter to work upon; to make a pin we must get copper, zinc, and tin out of mines; a ribbon requires the silk and the dye materials; everything that we touch, and use, and eat, and drink, contains substance, so that we must always begin by finding a supply of the right sort of materials.

Commonly, too, we want something more than matter; we want force which shall help us to carry and work the raw material. People naturally wish to avoid tiring themselves by labouring with their own arms and legs, and so they make windmills to grind corn, ships to carry goods, steam-engines to pump water and to do all sorts of hard work. From the earth, or, as we say, from Nature, we obtain both the materials of wealth and the force which helps us to turn the materials into wealth. Whatever thus furnishes us with the first requisite of production is called a **natural agent,** that is, something which acts for us and assists us (Latin, *agens,* acting). Among natural agents **land** is by far the most important, because, when supplied with abundant sunlight and moisture, it may be cultivated and made to yield all kinds of crops. Accordingly, economists often speak of land, when their remarks would really apply as well to rocks and rivers. Three-quarters of the whole surface of the globe is covered with seas; but this vast extent of salt water furnishes little wealth, except whales, seals, sea-weed, and a few other kinds of animals and plants. Hence, when we speak of land, we really mean any source of materials—any natural agent, and we may say that

land = source of materials = natural agent.

18. **Labour.** Nothing is more plain, however, than that natural agents alone do not make wealth. A man would perish in the most fertile spot if he did not take some trouble in appropriating the things around him. Fruit growing wild on the trees must be plucked before it becomes wealth, and wild game must be caught before it can be cooked and eaten. We must spend a great deal of labour if we wish to have comfortable clothes and houses and regular supplies of food; the proper sorts of materials must be gradually got together, and shaped and manufactured. Thus the amount of wealth which people can obtain depends far more upon their activity and skill in labouring than upon the abundance of materials around them.

As already remarked, North America is a very rich land, containing plenty of fine soil, seams of coal, veins of metal, rivers full of fish, and forests of fine timber, everything, in short, needed in the way of materials; yet the American Indians lived in this land for thousands of years in great poverty, because they had not the knowledge and perseverance to enable them to labour properly and produce wealth out of natural agents. Thus we see clearly that skilful and intelligent and regular labour is requisite to the pro- duction of wealth.

19. **Capital.** In order that we may produce much wealth, we require something further, namely, the **capital**, which supports labourers while they are engaged in their work. Men must have food once a day, not to say two or three times; if then they have no stock of food on hand, they must go at once and get it in the best way they can, for fear of starving. They must grub up roots, or gather grass seeds, or catch wild animals—if they can. When working in this way, they usually spend a great deal of labour for very little result; Australian natives sometimes have to cut down a large tree with stone axes, which is very hard work, in order to catch an opossum or two. Men who live in this way from hand to mouth have no time nor strength 'to make arrangements so as to get food and clothes in the easiest way. It requires much labour to plough the ground, to harrow it, and sow it with corn, besides fencing it in; when all this is done it is requisite to wait six months before the crop can be gathered. Certainly, the amount of food thus obtained is large compared with the labour: but wild Indians and other ignorant tribes of men cannot wait while the corn is growing; the poor Australian natives have to gather grass seeds or find worms and opossums every day.

There is a good Japanese maxim which says, " Dig a well before you are thirsty," and it is evidently very desirable to do so. But you must have capital to live upon while you are digging the well. In the same way, almost every mode of getting wealth without extreme labour requires that we shall have a stock of food to subsist upon while we are working and wait- ing, and this stock is called capital. In the absence of capital people find themselves continually in difficulties, and in danger of starvation. In the first of her tales·on political economy, called "Life in the Wilds," Miss Martineau has beautifully described the position of settlers at the Cape of Good Hope, who are imagined to have been attacked by Bushmen and robbed of their stock of capital. She shows us how difficult it is to get any food or to do any useful work, because something else is wanted beforehand—some tool, or material, or at any rate time to make it. But there is no time to make anything, because all attention has to be given to finding shelter for the night, and something for supper. Everybody who wishes to understand the necessity for capital, and the way capital serves us, should read this tale of Miss Martineau, and then go on to her other tales about Political Economy

We can hardly say that capital is as requisite to production as land and labour, for the reason that capital must have been the produce of land and labour. There must always, indeed, be a little capital in possession, even though it be only the last meal in the stomach, before we can produce more. But there is no good attempting to say exactly how capital began to be collected, because it began in the childhood of the world, when men and women lived more like wild animals than as we live now. Certain it is that we cannot have loaves of bread, and knives and forks, and keep ourselves warm with clothes and brick houses, unless we have a stock of capital to live upon while we are making all these things. **Capital is requisite, then, not so much that we shall labour, but that we shall labour economically and with great success.** We may call it a secondary requisite, and it would be best to state the requisites of production in this way—

Primary requisites...... $\begin{cases} \text{natural agent.} \\ \text{labour.} \end{cases}$

Secondary requisite.......capital.

20. **How to make Labour most Productive.** The great object must be to make labour as productive

as possible, that is, to get as much wealth as we can with a reasonable amount of labour. In order to do this we must take care to labour in the most favourable way, and there is no difficulty in seeing that we ought to labour

(1) **At the best time;**
(2) **At the best place;**
(3) **In the best manner.**

21. **Work at the best Time.** Of course we ought to do things when it is most easy to do them, and when we are likely to get most produce for our labour. The angler goes to the river in the early morning or the evening, when the fish will bite; the farmer makes hay while the sun shines; the miller grinds corn when the breeze is fresh, or the stream full; and the skipper starts when wind and tide are in his favour. By long experience farmers have found out the best time of year for doing every kind of work: seed is sown in autumn or spring; manure is carried in winter when the ground is frozen; hedges and ditches are mended when there is nothing else to do, and the harvest is gathered just when it is ripe, and the weather is fine. Norwegian peasants work hard all day in July and August to cut as much grass, and make as much hay as possible. They never think of timber then, because they know that there will be plenty of time during the long winter to cut down trees; and when the snow fills up all the hollows in the mountain side, they can easily drag the trees down to the rivers, which rise high with floods after the melting of the snow, and carry the logs away, without further labour, to the towns and ports. It is a good rule not to do to-day what we can probably do more easily to-morrow: but it is a still better rule not to put off till to-morrow what we can do more easily to-day. In order, however, that we may be able to wait and to do each kind of work at the best time, we must have enough **capital** to live upon in the meantime.

22. **Work at the Best Place.** Again, we

should carry on every kind of work at the place best suited for it, that we can get possession of. In many cases this is so obvious that the remark seems absurd. Does any one plant fruit trees on the sea sands, or sow corn among rocks? Of course not, because there would be no result. No one is so foolish as to spend his labour in a place where it would be wasted altogether. In other cases it is a question of degree; there may be some produce here, but there would be more produce there. In the south of England vines can be made to grow in the open air, and, in former days, wine used to be made from grapes grown in England. But vines grow much better on the sunny hills of France, Spain, and Germany, and the wine which can there be made with the same labour is far more plentiful and immensely better in quality. Those, then, who want to make wine had much better remove to the continent, or, still better, let the French, Spaniards, and Germans produce wine for us. In England we have good soil and a moist climate fitted for growing grass, and the best thing which our farmers can do is to raise cattle and produce plenty of milk, butter, and cheese.

In order that the world may grow as rich as possible, each country should give its attention to producing what it can produce most easily in its present circumstances, getting other things in exchange by foreign trade. The United States can raise endless quantities of cotton, corn, bacon, meat, fruit, petroleum, besides plenty of gold, silver, copper, iron, &c. Australia, New Zealand, and South Africa will furnish much wool, hides, sugar, preserved meats, besides gold, copper, and diamonds. Tropical Africa has palm oil, ivory, teak wood, gum, &c. South America abounds in cattle from which we get tallow, hides, bones, horns, essence of beef, &c. China supplies us with vast quantities of tea, in addition to silk, ginger, and many minor commodities. India sends cotton, indigo, jute, rice, seeds, sugar, spices, and all kinds of other products.   Every part of the world has some commodities which it can produce better than other countries, and if men and governments were wise, they would allow trade to be as free as possible, in order that each thing shall be produced where it costs the least labour to produce it.

23. **Work in the Best Manner.** Whatever the kind of industry carried on in a place, we ought to take care, thirdly, that each labourer works in the best manner, so as not to waste his labour or to make mistakes.   There are many different ways of setting about the same work, and, in order that he may choose the best, the labourer must be intelligent and skilful, or else he must be directed by some person who has knowledge and skill.   Moreover, there must be, as we shall see, great division of labour, so that each man shall do the kind of work he can do best. We need, then—

(1) **Science,**
(2) **Division of labour.**

24. **The Need of Science.**   In order that he may employ his labour to the best advantage, it is requisite that the labourer should be not merely skilful, that is, clever, and practised in handiwork, but that he should also be guided by a scientific knowledge of the things with which he is dealing.   Knowledge of nature consists, to a great extent, in understanding the **causes of things,** that is, in knowing what things must be put together in order that certain other things shall be produced.   Thus the steam-engine is due to the discovery that if heat be applied to water, the result is steam expanding with much force, so that a firebox, coal, boiler, and water are causes of force. Whenever we want to do any work, then, we must begin by learning, if possible, what are the causes which will produce it most easily and abundantly. By knowledge we shall often be saved from much needless labour.

As Sir John Herschel has explained, science some-

times shows us that **things which we wish to do
are really impossible,** as, for instance, to invent
a perpetual motion, that is, a machine which moves
itself.   At other times science teaches us that **the
way in which we are trying to make something is altogether the wrong way.**   Thus,
iron-masters used to think that the best way of smelt-
ing iron in the blast-furnace was to blow the furnace
with cold air ; science, however, showed that, instead
of being cold, the air sent into the furnace should be
made as hot as possible.   Then, again, science often
enables us **to do our work with a great saving
of labour.**   The boatman or bargeman takes care to
learn the state of the tide, so that he may have the
tide in his favour in making any journey.   Meteor-
ologists have now prepared maps of the oceans showing the sea-captain where he will find winds and cur-
rents most favourable to a rapid voyage.   Lastly,
**science sometimes leads us to discover
wonderful things which we should not have
otherwise thought it possible to do;** it is sufficient to mention the discovery of photography and
the invention of the telegraph and the telephone.   No
doubt it may be said that all the greatest improvements in industry—most of what tends to raise man
above the condition of the brute animals—proceed
from science.   The poet Virgil was right when he
said, **" Happy is he who knows the causes
of things."**

CHAPTER IV.

DIVISION OF LABOUR.

25. How Division of Labour Arises.   When
a number of workmen are engaged on any work, we
find that each man usually takes one part of the work,
and leaves other parts of the work to his mates.
People by degrees arrange themselves into different

trades, so that the whole work done in any place is divided into many employments or crafts. This division of labour is found in all civilised countries, and more or less in all states of society, which are not merely barbarous. In every village there is the butcher and the baker, and the blacksmith and the carpenter. Even in a single family there is division of labour: the husband ploughs, or cuts timber; the wife cooks, manages the house, and spins or weaves; the sons hunt or tend sheep; the daughters employ themselves as milkmaids. There is a popular couplet which says—

> "When Adam delved and Eve span,
> Who was then the gentleman?"

It seems to express the fact that this division of labour existed in very early times, before there were any gentlemen.

In modern times the division of labour is immensely complicated: not only has every town and village its different tradespeople, and artisans and men in different posts and employments, but each district has its peculiar manufactures. In one place cotton goods are produced; in another, woollen goods; in other parts of the country flax, jute, silk are manufactured. Iron is made in Staffordshire, Cleveland, South Wales, and Scotland; copper is smelted in South Wales; crockery is baked in the potteries; hosiery is manufactured in Nottingham and Leicester; linens are sewed in the North of Ireland; and so on. In every separate factory, again, there is division of labour; there is the manager, the chief clerk, the assistant clerks; the foremen of different departments, the timekeeper, the engine-tenter, and stokers, the common labourers, the carters, errand boys, porters, &c., all in addition to the actual mechanics of different kinds and ranks who do the principal work. Thus the division of labour spreads itself throughout the whole of society, from the Queen and her Ministers, down to the errand boy, or the street scavenger.

26. Adam Smith on the Division of Labour.
There are many ways in which we gain by the division
of labour, but Adam Smith has treated the subject so
excellently that we had better, in the first place,
consider his view of the matter. There are, as he
thought, three ways in which advantage arises from the
division of labour, namely—

(1.) Increase of dexterity in every particular workman.

(2.) Saving of the time which is commonly lost in
passing from one kind of work to another.

(3.) The invention of a great number of machines,
which facilitate and abridge labour, and enable one
man to do the work of many.

There can be no doubt as to the **increase of
dexterity,** which arises from practice. Any one who
has tried to imitate a juggler, or to play the piano,
without having learned to do it, knows how absurdly
he fails. Nobody could possibly do the work of a
glass-blower · without long practice. Even when a
man can do a job in some sort of way, he will do it
much more quickly if he does it often. Adam Smith
states that if a blacksmith had to make nails without
having been accustomed to the work, he would not
make above 200 or 300 bad nails in a day. With
practice he might learn to make 800 or 1000 nails in a
day ; but boys who are brought up to the nailer's trade
can turn out 2300 nails of the same kind in the same
time. But there is no need of many examples : everything that we see well or quickly made has been made
by men who have spent a great deal of time and trouble
in learning and practising the work.

Secondly, there is **a great deal of time lost
when a man changes from one kind of
work to another** many times in the day. Before you can make a thing you must get all
the right tools and materials around you ; when
you have finished one box, for instance, you are
all ready to make another with less trouble than the

first; but if you have to go off and do something quite different, such as to mend a pair of shoes or write a letter, a different set of implements have to be got ready. A man, as Adam Smith thought, saunters a little in turning his hand from one kind of employment to another, and if this happens frequently, he is likely to become lazy.

In the third place, Smith asserted that **the division of labour leads to the invention of machines** which abridge labour, because men, he thought, were much more likely to discover easy methods of attaining an object when their whole attention is directed to that object. But it seems doubtful how far this is correct. Workmen do occasionally invent some mode of lessening their labour, and a few important inventions have been made in this way. But, as a general rule, the division of labour leads to invention, because it enables ingenious men to make invention their profession. The greatest inventors, such as James Watt, Bramah, Fulton, Roberts, Nasmyth, Howe, Fairbairn, Whitworth, the Stephensons, Wheatstone, Bessemer, Siemens, have not been led to invention in the way described by Adam Smith, but have cultivated an original genius by careful study and long practice in mechanical construction. But the division of labour greatly assists invention, because it enables each factory to adopt particular kinds of machinery. In England the division of labour is continually becoming more and more minute, and it is not uncommon to find that the whole supply of some commodity is furnished from a single manufactory, which can then afford to have a set of machines invented on purpose to produce this one commodity. Such is even more the case in the large manufactories of the United States.

I will now describe four other ways in which great saving of labour arises from the division of labour, as follows :—

27. **The Multiplication of Services.** A great

deal of labour is often saved by arranging work so that a labourer may serve many persons as easily as one. If a messenger is going to carry a letter to the post-office, he can as readily carry a score. Instead of twenty people each carrying their own letters, one messenger can do the whole work without more trouble. This explains why the post-office is able to forward a letter from any part of the kingdom to any other part for a penny or even a halfpenny. There are so many people sending and receiving letters, that a postman usually carries a great many, and often delivers half-a-dozen at once. But it would be quite impossible to send telegrams so cheaply, because every message has to be separately telegraphed along the wires, and then delivered at once by a special messenger, who can seldom carry more than one message at a time. Archbishop Whately pointed out that when a party of travellers exploring a new country camp out at night, they naturally divide the work: one attends to the horses, another unpacks the stores, a third makes a fire and cooks the supper, a fourth goes for water, and so on. It would be quite absurd if a dozen travellers in one party were to light a dozen separate fires, and cook a dozen separate meals. The labour of lighting a fire and cooking for twelve persons is not much greater than doing the same for one or two. There are many things which, if once done, will serve for thousands or millions of people. If a person gets important information, as, for instance, that a storm is coming across the Atlantic Ocean, he can warn a whole nation by means of the newspapers. It is a great benefit to have a meteorological office in London, where two or three men spend their labour in learning the weather all over the country by means of the telegraph, and thus enable us to judge, as far as possible, of the weather which is coming. This is a good case of the **multiplication of services.**

28. **The Multiplication of Copies** is also a

means of increasing immensely the produce of labour. When the proper tools and models for making a thing are once provided, it is sometimes possible to go on multiplying copies with little further trouble. To cut the dies for striking a medal or coin is a very slow and costly work; but, when once good dies are finished, it is easy to strike a great many coins with them, and the cost of the striking is very small. The printing press, however, is the best case of multiplication of copies. To have the whole of Shakespeare's Plays copied out by a law stationer would cost more than two hundred pounds, and every new copy would cost as much as the first. Before the invention of printing, books used to be thus copied out, and manuscript books were therefore very expensive, besides being full of mistakes. The whole of Shakespeare's Plays can now be bought for a shilling; and any one of the Waverley Novels can be had for sixpence. It may cost several hundred pounds to set up the type for a large book and stereotype it; but when this is once done, hundreds of thousands of copies can be struck off, and the cost of each copy is little more than that of the paper and the binding.

Almost all the common things we use now, such as ordinary chairs and tables, cups and saucers, teapots, spoons and forks, &c., are made by machinery, and are copies of an original pattern. A good chair can be bought for five shillings or less, but if you wanted to have a chair made of a new pattern, it would cost perhaps five or ten times as much.

29. **Personal Adaptation.** A further advantage of the division of labour is that, when there are many different trades, every person can choose that trade for which he is best suited—the strong healthy man becomes a blacksmith; the weaker one works a loom or makes shoes; the skilful man learns to be a watchmaker; the most ignorant and unskilful can find work in breaking stones or mending the hedges. Each man will generally work at the trade in which he can get

the best wages, and it is an evident loss of skill if the artisan should break stones or sweep the streets. Now, the greater the division of labour and the more extensive factories become, the better chance there is for finding an employment just suited to each person's powers; clever workmen do the work which no one else can do; they have common labourers to help them in things which require no skill; foremen plan out the work, and allot it to the artisans; clerks, who are quick at accounts, keep the books, and pay and receive money; the manager of the factory is an ingenious experienced man, who can give his whole attention to directing the work, to making good bargains, or to inventing improvements in the business. Every one is thus occupied in the way in which his labour will be most productive and useful to other people, and at the same time most profitable to himself.

30. **Local Adaptation.** Lastly, the division of labour allows of local adaptation—that is, it allows every kind of work to be done in the place most suitable for it. We have already learnt (sec. 22, p. 29) that each kind of labour should be carried on where it is most productive; but this cannot be done unless there be division of labour—so that while the French grow wine, weave silk, or make *articles de Paris*, they buy the cottons of Manchester, the beer of Burton-on-Trent, or the coals of Newcastle. When trade is free, and the division of labour is perfect, each town or district learns to make some commodity better than other places: watches are made in Clerkenwell; steel pens in Birmingham; needles at Redditch; cutlery at Sheffield; pottery at Stoke; ribbons at Coventry; glass at St. Helen's; straw bonnets at Luton; and so forth.

It is not always possible to say exactly why certain goods are made better in one place—for instance, silks in Lyons—than anywhere else; but so it often is, and people should be left as free as possible to buy the goods they like best. Commodities are manufactured in order that they may produce pleasure and be useful, not, as we shall see, in order that labourers may be kept hard at work. Now, when trade is left free it gives rise to division of labour, not only between town and town, county and county, but between the most distant nations of the earth. Thus is created what may be called **the territorial division of labour.** Commerce between nation and nation is not only one of the best means of increasing wealth and saving labour, but it brings us nearer to the time when all nations will live in harmony, as if they were but one nation.

31. **The Combination of Labour.** We now see what great advantages arise from each man learning a single trade thoroughly. This is called the division of labour, because it divides up the work into a great many different operations ; nevertheless, it leads men to assist each other, and to work together in manufacturing the same goods. Thus, in producing a book, a great many trades must assist each other: type-founders cast the type ; mechanics make the printing press ; the paper is manufactured at the paper works ; printers' ink is prepared at other works ; the publishers arrange the business ; the author supplies the copy ; the compositors set up the type ; the reader corrects the proofs ; the pressmen work off the printed sheets ; then there are still the bookbinders, and the booksellers, besides a great many other small trades which supply the tools wanted by the principal trades. Thus, society is like a very complicated machine, in which there is a great number of wheels, and wheels within wheels ; each part goes on attending to its own business, and doing the same work over and over again. There is what we should call a **complex organization** (Greek, ὄργανον, instrument), that is to say, different people and different trades work as instruments of each other, all assisting in the ultimate result.

But it is to be observed that nobody plans out these systems of divided labour ; indeed few people ever know how many trades there are, and how they are connected together. There are said to be about thirty-six distinct kinds of employment in making and putting together the parts of a piano ; there are about forty trades engaged in watchmaking ; in the cotton business there are more than a hundred occupations. But new trades are frequently created, especially when any new discovery takes place ; thus, there are at least sixteen different trades occupied in photography, or in making the things required by photographers ; and railways have produced whole series of employments which did not exist fifty years ago. These trades arise without any Act of Parliament to make them or allow them. There is no law to say how many trades there shall be, nor how many people shall go into each trade, because nobody can tell what will be wanted in future years. These things are arranged by a kind of **social instinct.** Each person takes up the kind of work which seems to suit him and to pay him best at the time.

Another and a totally different kind of combination of labour arises when men arrange to assist each other in doing the same work. Thus, sailors pulling at the same rope combine their labour together ; other instances are, carrying the same ladder, rowing the same boat, and so forth. In this case there is said to be **simple combination of labour,** because the men do the same sort of work. When the men have different operations to perform, there is said to be **complex combination of labour,** as when one man points a pin and another makes the head. On board a ship there is both simple and complex combination. When several men work at the same capstan the combination is simple, because one man does exactly the same as the others. But the captain, mate, steersman, carpenter, boatswain, and cook work together in complex combination, since each attends to his own proper duties. Similarly, in a company of soldiers the privates act together in simple combination, but the officers of different ranks have distinct duties to perform, so that the combination becomes complex. Men who thus assist each other are usually able to do far more work than if they acted separately.

32. **Disadvantages of the Division of Labour.** There are certainly some evils which arise out of the great division of labour now existing in civilised countries. These evils are of no account compared with the immense benefits which we receive; still it is well to notice them.

In the first place, **division of labour tends to make a man's power narrow and restricted;** he does one kind of work so constantly, that he has no time to learn and practice other kinds of work. A man becomes, as it has been said, worth only the tenth part of a pin; that is, there are men who know only how to make, for instance, the head of a pin. In the time of the Romans it was said, *ne sutor ultra crepidam*, let not the shoemaker go beyond his last. When a man accustomed only to making pins or shoes goes into the far west states of America, he finds himself unfitted for doing all the kinds of hard work required from a settler. The poor peasant from Norway or Sweden, who seems at first sight a less intelligent man, is able to build his own house, till the ground, tend his horse, and in a rough way, make his own carts, implements, and household furniture. Even the Red Indian is much better able to take care of himself in a new country than the educated mechanic. The only thing to be said is that the skilled shoemaker, or mechanic of whatever sort, must endeavour to keep to the trade which he has learnt so well. It is a misfortune both for himself and for other people if he is obliged to undertake work which he cannot do so well.

A second disadvantage of the division of labour is that **trade becomes very complicated, and when deranged the results are ruinous to some people.** Each person learns to supply only a particular kind of goods, and if change of fashion

or any other cause leads to a falling off in the demand for that kind of goods, the producer is left in
poverty, until he can learn another trade.   At one
time the making of crinoline skirts for ladies was a
large and profitable trade; now it has ceased almost
entirely, and those who learnt the business have had
to seek other employments.   But each trade is generally well supplied with hands perfectly trained to the
work, and it is very difficult for fresh workmen,
especially when old, to learn the new work, and
compete with those who have long practised it.   In
some cases this has been successfully done; thus the
Cornish miners, when the mines in Cornwall were no
longer profitable, went into the collieries, where more
hewers of coal were much wanted.   But, generally
speaking, it is very difficult to find a new employment in England, and this is a strong reason why
trades-unions should make no objection to new men en-
tering a trade to which they have not been brought up.

The colliers tried to keep the Cornish miners out
of the coal pits.   In order to keep their own wages
as high as possible they would let other men starve.
But this is a very selfish and hurtful way of acting.
If every trade were thus to try and keep all other
people away, as if the trade were their own property,
there would constantly be a number of unfortunate
people brought to the workhouse through no fault of
their own.   It is most important, therefore, to maintain a man's right to do whatever kind of work he can
get.   It is one of the first and most necessary rights
of a labourer to labour in any honest way he finds
most profitable to himself.   **Labour must be free.**

CHAPTER V.

CAPITAL.

33. **What is capital?** We will now endeavour
to understand the nature of **the third requisite**

of production, called capital, which consists of wealth used to help us in producing more wealth. All capital is wealth,
but it is not true that all wealth is capital. If a man
has a stock of food, or a stock of money with which
he buys food, and he merely lives upon this without
doing any labour, his stock is not considered to be
capital, because he is not producing wealth in the
meantime. But if he is occupied in building a house,
or sinking a well, or making a cart, or producing anything which will afterwards save labour and give utility,
then his stock is capital.

The great advantage of capital is that it enables us
to do work in the least laborious way. If a man
wants to convey water from a well to his house, and
has very little capital, he can only get a bucket and
carry every bucket-full separately; this is very laborious. If he has more capital, he can get a barrel and
wheel it on a barrow, which takes off a large part of
the weight; thus he saves much labour by the labour
spent upon the barrel and barrow. If he has still
more capital his best way will be to make a canal, or
channel, or even to lay a metal pipe all the way from
the well to his house; this costs a great deal of labour
at the time, but, when once it is made, the water will
perhaps run down by its own weight, and all the rest
of his life he will be saved from the trouble of carrying water.

34. **Fixed and Circulating Capitals.** Capital
is usually said to be either fixed or circulating capital,
and we ought to learn very thoroughly the difference
between these two kinds. **Fixed capital** consists
of factories, machines, tools, ships, railways, docks,
carts, carriages, and other things, which last a long
time, and assist work. It does not include, indeed, all
kinds of fixed property. Churches, monuments, pictures, books, ornamental trees, &c., last a long time,
but they are not fixed capital, because they are not
used to help us in producing new wealth. They may

do good, and give pleasure, and they form a part of the wealth of the kingdom ; but they are not capital according to the usual employment of the name.

Circulating capital consists of the food, clothes, fuel, and other things which are required to support labourers while they are engaged in productive work. It is called circulating because it does not last long ; potatoes and cabbages are eaten up, and a new supply has to be grown ; clothes wear out in a few months or a year, and new ones have to be bought. The circulating capital, which is in the country now, is not the same circulating capital which was in the country two years ago. But the fixed capital is nearly the same : some factories may have been burnt or pulled down ; some machines may have become worn out, and have been replaced by new ones. But these changes in fixed capital are comparatively few ; whereas the whole or nearly the whole of the circulating capital is changed every year or two.

But the fact is that we cannot distinguish so easily as we may seem to do between fixed and circulating capitals ; there may be kinds of capital which are neither quite fixed nor quite circulating, but something between the two. Flour is soon eaten up, and is circulating capital. A flour mill lasts fifty years, perhaps, and may certainly be called fixed capital ; a flour sack lasts about ten years on an average. Is such a sack fixed or circulating capital ? It seems to me difficult to say. In the case of a railway, the coal and oil wanted for the engine are used up at once, and are clearly circulating capital ; the railway wagons last about ten years, the locomotive engines twenty years or more ; the railway stations last at least thirty years ; there is no reason why the bridges and tunnels and embankments should not last hundreds of years with proper care. Thus we see that **capital is altogether a question of time, and** we must say that capital is more fixed as it endures or continues useful a longer time; it is more circulating in proportion as it is sooner worn out or destroyed, and thus requires to be more frequently replaced.

35. How Capital is obtained. Capital is the result of saving or abstinence, that is, it can only be obtained by working to produce wealth, and then not immediately consuming that wealth. The poor savage who has to labour hard every day for fear that he may have to go without food, has no capital; but when he has food in hand, and can employ himself in making bows and arrows to facilitate the capture of animals, he is investing capital in the bows and arrows. Whenever we work in this way for a future purpose, we are living on capital and investing it. The abstinence (Latin, *abs*, from, and *tenens*, holding) consists in holding off from the enjoyment of something which we have produced, or might produce with the same labour. To save is to keep something whole or untouched for future use; we save it as long as we do not consume it. If I have a stock of flour and eat it up, there is an end of the flour, and I cannot be said to save that. But if, while eating the flour, I am engaged in making a plough or a cart, or any other durable thing which will help me in production, I have turned one form of capital into another form. I might have eaten the flour in idleness, in which case it would not have been capital. But, while eating it, I worked for a future purpose. In so doing I am said to invest capital, which means to turn circulating into fixed capital, or less durable into more durable capital. Capital, accordingly, is invested for longer or shorter periods according to the durability of the form in which it is invested (Latin, *in*, on, and *vestire*, to clothe). A good plough will perhaps last twenty years; all through that time the owner should be getting back by its use the benefit of the labour and

capital spent in making it. When it is worn out, he ought to have all the capital it cost paid back, with some increase or interest. Capital invested in railway wagons should pay itself back during the ten years that the wagons last on an average.

The capital invested in any work may always be said to consist of wages or what is bought with wages. Thus the capital invested in railways really consisted of the food, clothes, and other commodities consumed by the labourers who made the railways. It is true that tools also were needed as well as the iron rails, sleepers, bricks, and other materials required for the work. But as these things had previously been made by labour, we may consider that the capital really invested in them was the wages of the labourers who had already made them. Thus, **when we go far enough back, we always find that the capital invested consisted of the maintenance of labourers.**

36. **Investment of Capital.** We have two things to consider with regard to the investment of capital, **firstly, the quantity of the capital, and secondly, the length of time for which it is invested.** The same quantity of capital will keep more or less men at work, according as it is invested for shorter or longer periods. A man in growing potatoes only needs to wait for the result of his labour during one year on an average. If his food and clothing during one year cost thirty pounds, then capital worth thirty pounds is sufficient to keep him at work in this way. Three men cultivating potatoes will of course require three times as much capital, or ninety pounds worth; ten men will need three hundred pounds worth, and so on in proportion. But in growing vines it is necessary to wait several years after the vines are planted before they begin to bear. Suppose it to require five years waiting, then the labourer will want 5 × 30, or one hundred and fifty pounds worth of capital before he can grow vines. Three vine-growers

will want $3 \times 5 \times 30$, or four hundred and fifty pounds worth of capital; ten men, $10 \times 5 \times 30$, or fifteen hundred pounds worth, and so on in proportion. Thus we see clearly that the capital required in any kind of industry is proportional to the number of men employed, and also to the length of time for which the capital remains locked up, or invested on the average. But there is no fixed proportion whatever between the number of labourers and the capital they require—it entirely depends upon the length of time in which the capital is turned over, that is, invested, and got back again. A poor savage manages to live on a few days' capital in hand; a potato grower on one year's capital. On a modern farm in which many durable improvements are made, the quantity of capital required is very much greater. To employ men upon a railway requires immense capital, because so much of it is sunk in a very fixed and durable form in the embankments, tunnels, stations, rails, and engines.

37. **Labour cannot be Capital.** It is not uncommon to hear it said that **labour is the poor man's capital**; and then it is argued that the poor man has just as much right to live upon his capital as the rich man upon his. And so he has, if he can do it. If a labourer can go and produce any kind of wealth, and exchange it for food and necessaries, of course he may do so. But, as a general rule, he cannot do this without working for a length of time, waiting till the produce is finished and sold. In order to do this he wants something more than his labour, namely, his food in the meantime, besides materials and tools. These form the required capital, and there is no good in calling labour capital when it is really quite a different thing. At other times I have heard it said that **land is capital, intelligence is capital,** and so forth. These are all misleading expressions. The intended meaning seems to be that some people live upon what they get from land, or from intelligence, as other people live upon what they

5

get as interest upon capital. Nevertheless, land is not capital, nor is intelligence capital. Production requires, as we have seen, three distinct things, namely, land, labour, and capital ; and there is much harm in confusing things together by giving them the same name when they are not the same thing.

CHAPTER VI.

DISTRIBUTION OF WEALTH.

38. **How Wealth is Shared.** We have learned what wealth is, how it is to be used, and how it may be produced in the greatest quantities, with the least possible labour, but we have yet to enter on the more difficult parts of our subject. We must now try to make out how wealth is shared among those who have a hand in producing it. The requisites of production, as we have seen, are land, labour, and capital; if these were all supplied by the same person, no doubt the produce ought all to belong to him, with the exception of what is taken by the government as taxes. But, in a state of society such as exists at present, the labourer seldom owns all the land and capital he uses ; he goes to work on another man's farm, or in another man's factory ; he lives in another man's house, and often eats another man's food ; he derives benefits from other men's inventions, and discoveries ; and he uses roads, railways, public buildings, &c., furnished at the cost of the community.

The production of wealth, therefore, depends not on the will and exertions of a single man, but on the proper bringing together of land, labour, and capital, by different persons and classes of persons. These different persons must have their several shares of the wealth produced ; if they furnish something requisite for producing, they can make a bargain and ask for more or less of the produce. But **it is not mere chance or caprice which governs the sharing**

of wealth, and we have to learn the natural
laws according to which the distribution
takes place. We must ascertain how it is that many
of the population get so little, and some so much.
Men work very hard on a farm and raise crops; the
landlord ~~comes and~~ takes away a large part as rent,
so that the labourers have barely enough to live upon.
When we are able to understand why the labourer gets
so little at present, we shall see, perhaps, how he might
manage to get more, but in any case we shall see that
it is due in great part to the laws of nature.

The part of our subject which we are now going
to consider is called the **distribution of wealth**,
because it teaches us how the wealth produced is
distributed (Latin, *dis*, apart, and *tribuere*, to allot)
between the labourers, the owners of land, the owners
of capital, and the government. The part which the
labourer gets is called **wages**; the share of the land
owner is called **rent**; that of the capitalist is **interest**; and the government take **taxes**. We may
say that, as a general rule, the produce of work is
divided into four shares, which may be thus shown:

produce = wages + rent + interest + taxes.

39. **The Labourer's Share — Wages.** It
ought to be carefully remembered that the names
wages, rent, and **interest,** as here used, do not
exactly agree in meaning with the names as we employ them in common life. The wages paid to
workmen are sometimes more than wages, being
partly interest; the rent almost always consists partly
of interest; and what is called interest may in some
degree be really wages or rent.

By **wages** we mean, in political economy, nothing
but what goes to pay for the trouble of labour. But
many workmen own their own tools; masons have a
boxful of chisels, mallets, rules, &c..; carpenters often
require twenty or thirty pounds' worth of planes and
other implements; a pianoforte maker sometimes owns
seventy pounds' worth of tools; even gardeners re-

quire spades, rakes, a barrow, scythe, or perhaps a mowing machine and a roller. Now, all such tools represent so much invested capital, and a certain amount of interest must be paid for this capital. A pianoforte maker might expect five pounds a year as interest upon the cost of his tools. But true wages, are what remains after allowance has been made for such interest, and it would be proper to subtract also what is paid to the government as taxes.

40. **The Land Owner's Share—Rent,** the second part of the produce, means, in political economy, what is paid for the use of a natural agent, whether land, or beds of minerals, or rivers, or lakes. The rent of a house or factory is, therefore, not all rent in our meaning of the word. Capital has been spent in building the house or factory, and interest must be paid on this capital; we must then deduct this interest from what is commonly called the rent, before we can find out what is really rent. The ground rent of a house is the rent paid for the ground on which it stands, and this will be more nearly the true rent, apart from interest. Similarly, the ordinary rent of a farm will usually include interest upon the capital spent on the farm buildings, roads, gates, fences, drains, and other improvements. We shall afterwards learn exactly how true rent arises.

41. **The Capitalist's Share.** The proper share of the capitalist is **interest**; but this is usually a good deal less than what actually remains in the hands of the capitalist. Business is generally carried on by some capitalist who rents a piece of land, builds a factory, purchases machinery, and then employs men to work the machinery, paying them wages. The capitalist himself often acts as manager, and works every day almost as long as the workmen. When the goods are finished and sold, he keeps the whole of the money he gets for them; but then he has already paid out a large sum as wages, while the goods were being made; another part goes to pay the

rent of the land which he has hired. Having struck off these portions, there ought to remain a certain **profit,** part of which he uses to live upon. But even this profit consists of more than interest upon his capital. It should include also a payment for his labour in superintending the business. The manager of a factory may seldom touch the cotton, flax, iron, or other material, which is manufactured; nevertheless, he works with his head and his pen, calculating the prices at which he can produce goods, inquiring where he can buy the materials most cheaply, choosing good workmen, keeping the accounts straight, and so on. Severe mental labour is really far more difficult and exhausting than manual labour; and in raising up a good business, and carrying it through times of danger, a manager has to undergo great anxiety and mental fatigue. Thus, it is necessary that a successful manager should receive a considerable share of the produce, so as to make it worth his while to give this labour. His share is called **the wages of superintendence,** and, although usually much larger than the share of a common labourer, it is really wages of the same nature.

Another part of the capitalist's so-called profit ought to be laid aside as **recompense for risk.** There is always more or less uncertainty in trade, and even the most skilful and careful manager may lose money by "circumstances over which he has no control." Sometimes, after building a factory, the demand for the goods which he is going to produce falls off; sometimes the materials cannot be bought; perhaps it is discovered, when too late, that the factory has been built in an unsuitable place; occasionally, too, the workmen are discontented, and refuse to work for such wages as the capitalist can afford to pay. Now, whenever any of these mistakes or misfortunes happen, it is the capitalist who mainly suffers, because he loses a great deal of money, on which he might otherwise have lived comfortably. Sometimes men who have worked hard all their lives, and grown rich by degrees, lose all their wealth again in the end, by some error of judgment or by some unfortunate event due to no fault of their own.

A capitalist, then, must have some inducement for running into these disagreeable risks; by lending his capital to the government he might get interest for it, and be nearly sure not to lose. If, then, he puts it into trade, and runs the risk of loss, he must have a recompense for the risk. This ought to be at least enough to make the profits of the successful business balance the losses of the unfortunate ones, so that on the average capitalists will get the interest of capital and the wages of superintendence free from loss. We may say, then, that—

profit = wages of superintendence
+ interest + recompense for risk.

42. **About Interest.** That which is paid for the use of capital altogether apart from what is due for the trouble and risk of the person conducting the business, is called **interest**. This interest, of course, will be greater or less according as the amount of capital is greater or less; it will also be greater or less according as the capital is employed for a longer or shorter time. Thus the rate of interest is always stated in proportion to the capital sum and to the time; *five per cent. per annum* means that, for every hundred pounds of capital, five pounds are paid during every year in which the capital is used, and in the same proportion for longer or shorter times.

The rates of interest actually paid in business vary very much, from one or two per cent. up to fifty per cent. or more. When the rate is above five or six per cent., it will be to some extent not true interest, but compensation for the risk of losing the capital altogether. To learn the true average rate of interest, we must inquire what is paid for money lent to those who are sure to pay it back, and who give property in pledge, so that there may be no doubt about the matter. It seems probable that the true average ⟩ rate of interest in England is at present about four per cent., but it varies in different countries, being lower in England and Holland than anywhere else. In the United States it is probably six or seven per cent.

The most important fact about **interest** is that **it is ⟩ the same in one business as in another.** The rates of profit differ very much, it is true, but this is because the labour of superintendence is different, or because there is greater risk in one trade than another. But the true interest is the same, because capital, being lent in the form of money, can be lent to one trade just as easily as to another. There is nothing in circulating capital which fits it for one trade more than another : accordingly it will be lent to that trade which offers ever so little more interest than other trades. Thus **there is a constant tendency to** ⟩ **the equality of interest in all branches of industry.**

CHAPTER VII.

WAGES.

43. **Money Wages and Real Wages.** Wages, as we have already learnt, are the payments received ⟩ by a labourer in return for his labour. It does not matter whether these payments are received daily, weekly, monthly, quarterly, or yearly. A day gardener is, perhaps, paid every evening ; an artisan is usually paid on Saturday or Friday night, or sometimes fortnightly ; clerks receive their salaries monthly ; managers, officers, secretaries, and others, are paid quarterly, or sometimes half-yearly. When the wages are paid monthly, or at longer intervals, they are generally ⟩ called **salary** (Latin, *salarium*, money given to Roman soldiers for salt) ; but if the salary is paid for labour and nothing else, it is exactly the same in nature as wages.

I said, in the last chapter, that wages consist of a share of the produce of labour, land, and capital; in the preceding paragraph, I have been saying that it consists of payments. Here arises one of the great difficulties of our subject. As a matter of fact, the wages received by labourers, in the present day, consist almost always of money. A person working in a cotton mill produces cotton yarn; but he does not receive at the end of the week so much cotton yarn; he receives so many shillings. This is much more convenient; for if the labourer received cotton yarn, or any other commodity which he produces, he would have to go and sell it in order to buy food and clothes, and to pay the rent of his house. Instead, then, of receiving an actual share of the produce, he receives from the capitalist as much money as is supposed to be equal in value to his share.

Now, we shall see that it is requisite to distinguish between **money wages** and **real wages**. What a labourer really works for is the bread, clothes, beer, tobacco, or other things which he consumes; these form the real wages. If he gets more of these, it does not matter whether he gets more or less money wages; he cannot eat money, or use it in any way except to spend it at shops. If corn or cotton becomes dearer, the wages of every workman are really lessened; because he can buy less corn or cotton with his money wages. On the other hand, everything which makes goods cheaper, increases the real wages of workmen; because they can get more of the goods in exchange for the same money wages. People are accustomed to think far too much about the number of shillings they get for a day's work; they fancy that, if they get 25 per cent. more money wages, they must be 25 per cent. more wealthy. But this is not necessarily the case; for if the prices of goods on the average have also risen 25 per cent., they will be really no richer nor poorer than before.

We now begin to see that to increase the produc-

tiveness of labour is really the important thing for
everybody.   For if anything, such as cotton cloth,
can be made with less labour, it can be sold more
cheaply, and everybody can buy more of it for the
same money, and thus be better clothed.   If the same
were the case with other goods, so that linen, stock-
ings, boots, bricks, houses, chairs, tables, clocks, books,
&c., were all made in larger quantities than before,
with the same labour, everybody in the country would
be better supplied with the things which he really
wishes to have.

   It is certain that **a real increase of wages to**
the people at large is to be obtained only by
making things cheaply.   No doubt a tradesman
gains sometimes when the goods he deals in become
dearer, but to the extent that they are dearer, all
consumers of the goods lose, because they can enjoy
less comforts and necessaries.   But, if goods are made
cheaply, all consumers gain thereby, and, all people
being consumers, all gain so far as they use the
cheapened articles.   Nor does it follow that artisans
and tradespeople suffer by the cheapening of goods.
If, owing to some invention, much greater quantities are made with the same labour, the artisan
will probably be able to sell his share of the produce
for more than before, that is, his wages will rise instead
of falling by the cheapening of the produce.   The
tradesman, again, may gain less on each separate
article that he sells, but he may sell so much more
than before, that his total profits may be increased.
The result to which we come is, then, that **all**
increase of produce, and cheapening of goods
tends to the benefit of the public, and this is
the true way in which people are made
richer.

   44. **How Differences of Wages arise.**   It is
very important to understand rightly the reasons of the
great differences which exist between the rates of
wages paid in different occupations.   Some kinds of

labourers are paid a hundred or even a thousand times as much for a day's work as others, and it may seem very unfair that there should be such great differences. We must learn to see that this is the necessary result of the various characters and abilities of persons, partly arising from the actual strength of mind and body with which they were born, partly from the opportunities of education and experience which they have happened to enjoy. We are often told that all men are born free and equal; however this may be in a legal point of view, it is not true in other ways. One child is often strong and stout from its earliest years; another weakly and unfit for the same exertion. In mind there are still more remarkable differences.

The rates of wages in different employments are governed by **the laws of supply and demand** which we shall afterwards consider. Just as goods rise in price when there is little in the market and much is wanted, so the price of men's labour rises when much of any particular kind is wanted and little is to be had. It does not matter much whether we speak of demand for goods or demand for the labour, which is necessary to make the goods. If more things of a certain sort are wanted, then more men able to make them must be found. If I buy an aneroid barometer, I use up the labour of a man able to make such a barometer; if many people take a fancy to have aneroid barometers, and only a few workmen have the necessary skill to make them, they can ask a high price for their labour. It is true that people buying barometers do not usually pay the workmen for making them; a man with capital gets the barometers made beforehand and puts them in shops ready for sale. The capitalist advances the wages of the workmen, but this is only for a few weeks or months, and according as the demand for barometers is brisk or slow, he employs more or fewer workmen. Thus, **demand for commodities comes to nearly, though not quite, the same thing as demand**

for labour. There is the profit of the capitalist to be considered as well; but, with this exception, **rates of wages are governed by the same laws of supply and demand as the prices of goods.**

Anything, then, which affects the numbers of men able and willing to do a particular kind of work, affects the wages of such men. Thus the principal circumstance governing wages is the comparative numbers of persons brought up with various degrees of strength, both of body and mind. The greater number of ordinary men, while in good health, have sufficient strength of arms and legs to do common work; the supply of such men is consequently very large, and, unless they can acquire some peculiar knowledge or skill, they cannot expect high wages. Dwarfs and giants are always much less common than men of average size; if there happened to be any work of importance which could only be done by dwarfs or giants, they could demand high wages. Dwarfs, however, are of no special use except to exhibit as curiosities; very large strong men, too, are not generally speaking of any particular use, because most heavy work is now done by machinery. They can, however, still get very high wages in hewing coal, or puddling iron, because this is work, requiring great strength and endurance, which is not yet commonly done by machinery. Iron puddlers sometimes earn as much as £250 a year.

It is great skill and knowledge which generally enable a man to earn large wages. Rich people like to get the best of everything, and thus the few people who can do things in the best possible way can ask very high prices. Almost any one can sing badly; but hardly any one can sing as well as Mr. Sims Reeves: thus he can get perhaps £20 or £30 for every song which he sings. It is the same with the best artists, actors, barristers, engineers. An artist is usually his own capitalist, for he maintains himself dur-

ing many months, or even years, while he is painting a
great picture ; if he succeeds in doing it excellently
well, he can sell the picture for thousands of pounds,
because there are many rich people who wish to
possess good pictures.

45. **Adam Smith on Wages.**   There are, however, various circumstances which cause wages in any
particular employment to be higher or lower than in
other employments, and we had better attend to what
Adam Smith has said on this subject.   He mentioned
five principal circumstances which make up for small
wages in some occupations, and balance great wages
in other ones, as follows :

(1.) **The Agreeableness or Disagreeableness
of the Employments themselves.**   If an employment is in itself comparatively pleasant, it attracts
many who would not otherwise go into it at the
current wages.   Thus, officers of the army and navy
are not on the average highly paid ; but there is never
any difficulty in finding men willing to be officers,
because the work is thought to be easy, and there is
honour and power attaching to it.   On the other
hand, a good butcher makes high wages, because his
business is a greasy one, besides being thought to be
cruel, and a clever man must be attracted to it by
good earnings.

(2.) **The Easiness and Cheapness, or the
Difficulty and Expense of learning the Occu-
pation.**   This circumstance always has much importance, because the greater number of the people are
poor, and are consequently unable to give their
children a long good education.   Thus, the larger
part of the young men who grow up are only fit for
common manual employments, and therefore get low
wages.   To learn a profession, like that of an architect
or engineer, it is requisite to pay a high premium, and
become a pupil in a good office, and then there are
many years to be spent in practising and waiting
before profit begins to be made.   Hence the com-

paratively few who succeed in the difficult professions gain very high wages.

(3.) **The Constancy or Inconstancy of Employment.** When a man is sure of being employed and paid regularly all the year round, he is usually willing on that account to accept a less rate of wages. Thus, there is little difficulty in finding men to be policemen at about 25 shillings a week; for though they have to go on duty at night, and their work is often tedious and disagreeable, yet policemen are nearly sure to have employment as long as they behave well. A carpenter or bricklayer, on the contrary, is sometimes thrown out of work, and becomes anxious as to the means of keeping his family. Masons and bricklayers, who cannot work during frosty weather, ought of course to have higher wages during the rest of the year, so as to make up a good average. Dock-labourers, who are simply strong men without any particular skill, earn large wages when trade is brisk and many ships come into the docks; at other times, when trade is slack, or when contrary winds keep ships out of port, they often fall into destitution through want of employment.

(4.) **The Small or Great Trust which must be reposed in those who exercise the Employments.** This circumstance considerably affects the supply of people suitable for certain occupations. A man cannot expect to get employment in a bank, or in a jeweller's shop, unless he has a good character. Nothing is more difficult than for a person convicted of dishonesty to find desirable employment. Thus, a good character is often worth a great deal of money. Honesty, indeed, is so far common that it does not alone command high wages; but it is one requisite. The cleverest man would never be made the manager of a large business, if there was reason to think that he had committed fraud.

(5.) Lastly, **The Probability or Improbability of Success in Employments greatly affects** the **Wages of those who succeed.** In some cases, a man can hardly avoid succeeding; if he once enlists, he is made into a soldier whether he likes it or not. Almost all, too, who become clerks in banks, counting-houses, or public offices, can succeed in doing some of the work required in such offices. Accordingly clerks are seldom highly paid. But of those who become barristers, only a few have the peculiar knowledge, tact, and skill required to make them successful; these few make very large gains, and the unsuccessful men have to seek for other employments.

Some occupations are very badly paid, because they can be taken up by men who fail in other work. Frequently a person who has learnt a trade or profession finds that he is unfit for it; in other cases, there is a failure in the demand for a commodity, which obliges its manufacturers to seek other work. Such people are usually too old and too poor to begin again from the beginning, and learn a new difficult trade. Thus they have to take to the first work they can do. Educated men who have not been successful become secretaries, house-agents, insurance-agents, small wine merchants, and the like. Uneducated men have to drive cabs, or go into the army, or break stones; poor women become seamstresses, or go out charing. Here again we see the need of leaving everybody at perfect liberty to enter any trade which he can manage to carry on; it is not only injurious to the public, but it is most unfair to people in misfortune, if they are shut out of employments by the artificial restrictions of those who already carry on those employments.

46. **What is a Fair Day's Wages?** It is a favourite saying that **a man should have a fair day's wages for a fair day's work; but this is a fallacious saying.** Nothing, at first sight, can seem more reasonable and just; but when you examine its meaning, you soon find that there is no real meaning at all. It amounts merely to saying, that

a man ought to have what he ought to have. There is no way of deciding what is a fair day's wages. Some workmen receive only a shilling a day; others two, three, four, or five shillings; a few receive as much as ten, or even twenty shillings a day; which of these rates is fair? If the saying means that all should receive the *same* fair wages, then all the different characters and powers of men would first have to be made the same, and exactly equalised. We have seen that wages vary according to the laws of supply and demand, and as long as workmen differ in skill, and strength, and the kind of goods they can produce, there must be differences of demand for their products. Accordingly, there is no more a fair rate of wages than there is a fair price of cotton or iron. It is all a matter of bargain; he who has corn or cotton or iron or any other goods in his possession, does quite right in selling it for the best price he can get, provided he does not prevent other people from selling their goods as they think best. So, any workman does quite right in selling his labour for the highest rate of wages he can get, provided that he does not interfere with the similar right of other workmen to sell their labour as they like.

CHAPTER VIII.

TRADES-UNIONS.

47. **The Purposes of Trades-Unions.** Working-men commonly think that the best way to raise their earnings is to form trades-unions, and oblige their employers to pay better wages. **A trades-union is a society of men belonging to any one kind of trade, who agree to act together as they are directed by their elected council, and who subscribe money to pay the expenses.** Some trades-unions are very different from

others, and they are not all well conducted nor all
badly conducted, any more than people are all well
behaved or all badly behaved. Moreover, the same
trades-union often does different kinds of business.
Usually they act as benefit or friendly societies, that
is to say, if a member of a trades-union pays his sub-
scription of say one shilling weekly, together with an
entrance-fee and other small payments, he has a right,
after a little time, to receive say twelve shillings a
week in case of illness ; he gets back the value of his
tools if they should happen to be burnt or lost ; when
thrown out of work he will enjoy say ten shillings a
week for a certain length of time ; if he is so unfortunate as to be disabled by accident, he receives a
good sum of money as an accident benefit; and when
he dies he is buried at the expense of the union. All
these arrangements are very good, for they insure a
man against events which are not usually under his
own control, and they prevent workmen from becoming paupers. So far as trades-unions occupy themselves in this way, it is impossible not to approve of
them very warmly.

Then, again, trades-unions are able to take care of
their members by insisting that employers shall make
their factories wholesome and safe. If a single workman were to complain that the workshops were too
hot, or that a machine was dangerous, or a mine not
properly ventilated, he would probably not be listened
to, or would be told to go about his business. But if
all the workmen complain at once, and let it be
known that they do not intend to go on working
unless things are made better, the employer will think
about the matter seriously, and will do anything that
is reasonable to avoid disputes and trouble. Everybody is justified in taking good care of his own life
and health, and in making things as convenient to
himself as possible. Therefore we cannot find fault
with workmen for discussing such matters among
themselves, and agreeing upon the improvements they

think right to demand. It is quite proper that they should do so.

But nobody is perfectly wise, and those who have not much time to get knowledge, and learn science and political economy, will often not see the effects of what they demand. They may ask for something which is impossible, or would cost so much as to stop the trade altogether. In all such matters, therefore, working-men should proceed cautiously, hearing what their employers have to say, and taking note especially of what the public opinion is, because it is the opinion of many who have nothing to lose or gain in the matter.

48. **The Regulation of Hours.** One of the principal subjects of dispute is usually the number of hours in the day that a workman should work. In some trades a man is paid by the hour or by the work done, so that each man can labour a longer or shorter time as he prefers. When this is the case, each man is the best judge of what suits him, and no trades-union ought to interfere. But in factories, generally speaking, it would not do to let the men come and go when they liked; they must work while the engines and machines are moving, and while other men need their assistance. Accordingly, somebody must settle whether the factory is to work for twelve, or ten, or nine, or eight hours a day. The employer would generally prefer long hours, because he would get more work and profit out of his buildings and machines, and he need not usually be on the spot all the time himself. It seems reasonable, then, that the workmen should have their opinion, and have a voice in deciding how long they will work.

But workmen are likely to be mistaken, and imagine that they may get as much wages for nine hours' work as for ten. They think that the employer can raise the price of his goods, or that he can well afford to pay the difference out of his own great profits. But if political economy is to be believed, the wages of workmen are really the value of the goods produced, after the necessary rent of land and interest of capital have been paid.   If factories, then, produce less goods in nine hours than in ten, as is usually the case, there cannot, in the long run, be so much wages to receive.   On the other hand, as machinery is improved, labour becomes more productive, and it is quite right that those who are sufficiently well paid should prefer, within reasonable limits, to lessen their hours of work rather than increase their earnings. This is a matter which depends upon many considerations, and it cannot be settled in this Primer.   What I should conclude is, that when workmen want to lessen their hours of work, they ought not to ask the same wages for the day's work as before.   It is one thing to lessen the hours of work ; it is another thing to increase the rate of wages per hour, and though both of these things may be rightly claimed in some circumstances, they should not be confused together.

49. **The Raising of Wages.**   The principal object of trades-unions, however, is to increase the rate of wages.   Working men seem to believe that, if they do not take care, their employers will carry off the main part of the produce, and pay very low wages. They think that capitalists have it all their own way unless they are constantly watched, and obliged to pay by fear of strikes.   Employers are regarded as tyrants who can do just as they like.   But this is altogether a mistake.   No capitalists can for more than a year or two make unusual profits, because, if they do, other capitalists are sure to hear of it, and try to do likewise.   The result will be that the demand for labourers in that kind of trade will increase ; the capitalists will bid against each other for workmen, and they will not, generally speaking, be able to get enough without raising the rate of wages.

There is no reason whatever to think that trades-unions have had any permanent effect in raising wages in the majority of trades.   No doubt wages are now much higher than they were thirty or forty years ago; but to a certain extent this is only a rise of money wages, due to the abundance of gold discovered in California and Australia. The rest of the increase can be easily accounted for by the great improvements in machinery, and the general prosperity of the country. It is certain, too, that the increase of wages is not confined to those trades which have unions; even common labourers who have no unions receive considerably more money wages than they did, and domestic servants, who never strike in a body, but simply leave one place when they can get a better, have raised their own wages quite as much as any union could have done it for them.

50. **Strikes and Lockouts. Workmen are said to strike, that is, to strike work, when a number of them agree together to cease working on a certain day for certain employers,** in order to oblige these employers to pay better wages, or in some way to yield to their demands. When one or more employers suddenly dismiss their workpeople altogether, in order to oblige them to take lower wages, or agree to some alteration of work, it is called **a lockout, and a lockout is nearly the same as a strike of the employers.** Strikes sometimes last for many months, the workmen living on what savings they have, and on contributions sent to them by workmen or unions in the same or other trades. The employers at the same time lose much money by their factories standing still, and they sometimes receive aid from other employers.

There is nothing legally or morally wrong in a strike or lockout when properly conducted. A man, when free from promises or contracts, has a right to work or not to work, as he thinks best, that is to say, the law regards it as beneficial to the country, on the whole, that people should be free to do so. Similarly, employers are free to work their mills or not as they like.

engagements; men who have promised to work to the end of the week must of course do so; they are not free till their promise is performed. Again, nobody should be allowed suddenly to stop work in a way endangering other people. Enginedrivers and guards in America sometimes strike when a train is halfway on its journey, and leave the passengers to get to the next town as they best can. This is little better than manslaughter. Neither the owners nor the workmen in gasworks, waterworks, or any other establishment on which the public depends for necessaries of life, should be allowed suddenly to stop work without notice. The safety of the public is the first considera-tion. The law ought therefore to punish those who make such strikes.

51. **The General Effect of Strikes.** There is not space in this little work to argue the matter out in detail, but I have not the least doubt that **strikes, on the whole, produce a dead loss of wages to those who strike, and to many others.** I believe that if there had not been a strike during the last thirty years, wages would now be higher in general than they are, and an immense amount of loss and privation would also have been saved. It has, in fact, been shown by Dr. John Watts of Manchester, in his "Catechism of Wages and Capital," that even a suc-cessful strike usually occasions loss. He has said, "Allowing for accidental stoppages, there will not be in the most regular trades above fifty working weeks in the year, and one week will therefore represent two per cent. of the year. If a strike for four per cent. rise on wages succeeds in a fortnight, it will take twelve months' work at the improved rate to make up for the lost fortnight; and if a strike for eight per cent. lasts four weeks, the workmen will be none the richer at the end of twelve months'; so that it frequently happens that, even when a strike succeeds, another revision of wages takes place before the last loss is made up; a successful strike is, therefore, like a suc-

cessful lawsuit—only less ruinous than an unsuccessful one." If we remember that a large proportion of strikes are unsuccessful, in which case of course there is simple loss to every one concerned ; that when successful, the rise of wages might probably have been gradually obtained without a strike ; that the loss by strikes is not restricted to the simple loss of wages, but that there is also injury to the employers' business and capital, which is sure to injure the men also in the end ; it is impossible to doubt that the nett result of strikes is a dead loss. The conclusion to which I come is that, **as a general rule, to strike is an act . of folly.**

52. **Intimidation in Strikes.** Those who strike work have no right to prevent other workmen from coming and taking their places. If there are unemployed people, able and willing to work at the lower wages, it is for the benefit of everybody, excepting the strikers, that they should be employed. It is a question of supply and demand. The employer, generally speaking, is right in getting work done at the lowest possible cost ; and, if there is a supply of labour forthcoming at lower rates of wages, it would not be wise of him to pay higher rates.

But it is unfortunately common for those who strike to endeavour to persuade or even frighten workmen from coming to take their places. This is as much as to claim a right to the trade of a particular place, which no law and no principle gives to them. A strike is only proper and legal as long as it is entirely voluntary on the part of all concerned in refusing to work. When a striker begins to threaten or in any way prevent other people from working as they like, he commits a crime, by interfering with their proper liberty, and at the same time injuring the public. Men are free to refuse to labour, but it is absolutely necessary to maintain at the same time the freedom of other men to labour if they like. The same considerations, of course, apply to lockouts ; no employer who locks out his workmen has any right to intimidate, or in any way to oblige other employers to do the same. No doubt voluntary agreements are made between employers, and lockouts are jointly arranged, just as extensive strikes are arranged beforehand. If any employers were to go beyond this and threaten to injure other employers if they did not join in the lockout, they should be severely punished. But such a case seldom or never occurs. Thus, strikes and lockouts are proper only as mere trials, to ascertain whether labour will be forthcoming at a certain rate of wages, or under certain conditions.

If the workmen in a trade are persuaded that their wages are too low, then a strike will show whether it is the case or not; if their employers find themselves unable to get equally good workmen at the same wages, they will have to offer more; but if equally good can be got at the old rate, then it is a proof that the strikers made a mistake. Their wages were as good as the state of trade warranted. It is all a matter of bargain, and of supply and demand. Those who strike work are in the position of those who, having a stock of goods, refuse to sell it, hoping to get a better price. If they make a mistake, they must suffer for it, and those who choose to sell their goods in the meantime will have the benefit. But it is plain that it would never do to allow one holder of goods to intimidate and prevent other holders from selling to the public. It is worthy of consideration whether even voluntary combinations of dealers should not be prohibited, because they are often little better than conspiracies to rob the public. The good of consumers, that is, of the whole people, is what we must always look to, and this is best secured when men act freely and compete with each other to sell things at the cheapest rates.

53. **Trades-Union Monopolies.** It cannot be denied that, in certain trades, the men may succeed to some extent in keeping their wages above the natural level by union. Wages, like the prices of goods, are

governed by the laws of supply and demand. Accordingly, if the number of hat-makers can be kept down it reduces the number of hats that can be made, raises their prices, and enables the hat-makers to demand higher wages than they otherwise could do. Many unions try thus to limit production by refusing to admit more than a fixed number of apprentices, and by declining to 'work with any man who has not been brought up to the trade. It is probable that, where a trade is a small one, and the union powerful, there may be some success. The trade becomes a monopoly, and gets higher wages by making other people pay dearer for the goods they produce. They raise a tax from the rest of the nation, including all the workmen of other trades. This is a thoroughly selfish and injurious thing, and the laws ought by all reasonable means to discourage such monopolies. Moreover, monopoly is extremely hurtful in the long run to the working classes, because all the trades try to imitate those which are successful. Finding that the hatters have a strong union, the shoemakers, the tailors, and the seamstresses try to make similar unions, and to restrict the numbers employed. If they could succeed in doing so, the result would be absurd ; **they would all be trying to grow richer by beggaring each other.** As I have pointed out in the *Logic Primer* (section 177, p. 117), this is a logical fallacy, arising from the confusion between a general and a collective term. **Because any trade separately considered may grow richer by taxing other trades, it does not follow that all trades taken together, and doing the same thing, can grow richer.**

No doubt, working men think that, when their wages are raised, the increase comes out of the pockets of their employers. But this is usually a complete mistake ; their employers would not carry on business unless they could raise the prices of their goods, and thus get back from purchasers the increased sum which

they pay in wages. They will even want a little more
to recompense them for the risk of dealing with
workmen who strike at intervals, and thus interrupt
business. It is the consumers of goods who ultimately
pay the increased wages, and though wealthy peopl⸱
no doubt pay a part of the cost, it is mainly the
working people who contribute to the higher wages of
some of their own class.

The general result of trades-union monopolies to the
working people themselves is altogether disastrous. If
one in a hundred, or one in a thousand is benefited,
the remainder are grievously injured. The restrictions
upon work which they set up tend to keep men from
doing that which they are ready and willing to do.
The lucky fatten at the cost of those whom they shut
out in want of work, and the strikes and interruptions
of trade, occasioned by efforts to keep up monopolies,
diminish the produce distributed as wages.

54. **Professional Trades-Unions.** We often
hear the proceedings of trades-unions upheld on the
ground that lawyers, doctors, and other professional
men have their societies, Inns of Court, or other unions,
which are no better than trades-unions. This is what
may be called a *tu quoque* (thou also) argument. "We
may form unions because you form unions." It is a
poor kind of argument at best; one man acting un-
wisely is no excuse for another doing so likewise. I
am quite willing to allow that many of the rules of
barristers and solicitors are no better than those of
trades-unions. That a barrister must begin to be a
barrister by eating certain dinners; that he must never
take a fee under a certain amount; that he must never
communicate with a client except through a solicitor;
that a senior counsel must always have a junior; and
most of the rules of the so-called **etiquette** are clearly
intended to raise the profits of the legal profession.
Many things of this kind want reform. But, on the
other hand, these unions avoid many of the faults of
trades-unions. There is no limit to the number of

persons who may enter them; all men of good character and sufficient knowledge can become barristers and solicitors. Moreover, the entrance to the legal, medical, and several other professions is being more and more regulated by examinations, which are intended purely to secure able men for the service of the public. Nor is any attempt made in these professional trades-unions to prevent men from exerting themselves as much as they can, so as to serve the public to the utmost of their ability. These professional trades-unions are thus free from *some* of the evils which other unions produce.

55. **The Fallacy of Making Work.** One of the commonest and worst fallacies into which people fall in political economy is to imagine that wages may be increased by doing work slowly, so that more hands shall be wanted. Workmen think they see plainly that the more men a job requires, the more wages must be paid by their employers, and the more money comes from the capitalists to the labourers. It seems, therefore, that any machine, invention, or new arrangement which gets through the work more quickly than before, tends to decrease their earnings. With this idea, bricklayers' labourers refuse (or did lately refuse) to raise bricks to the upper parts of a building by a rope and winch; they preferred the old, laborious, and dangerous mode of carrying the bricks up ladders in hods, because the work then required more hands. Similarly, brickmakers refused to use any machinery; masons totally declined to set stones shaped and dressed by machinery; some compositors still object to work in offices where type-composing machines are introduced. They are all afraid that if the work is done too easily and rapidly, they will not be wanted to do it; they think that there will be more men than there are berths for, and so wages will fall. In almost every case this is an absurd and most unfortunate mistake.

No doubt, if men insist on sticking to a worse way of doing work after a better one has been invented, they may get bad wages, and perhaps go to the work-house in old age. Thus, the hand-weavers in Spital-fields would continue weaving by hand, instead of learning to weave by steam power, and the case is somewhat the same with the hand-nailers of South Staffordshire. But when the younger workmen of a trade are wise and foreseeing enough to adopt a new invention as soon as it is successful, they are never injured, and usually much benefited by it. Seam-stresses in England received wretchedly poor wages before the introduction of the American sewing machine, and they thought they would be starved altogether when the same work could be done twenty times as fast by machine as by hand. The effect, however, has been just of the opposite kind. Those who were not young, skilful or wise enough to learn machine-sewing, receive better wages for hand-sewing than they would formerly have done. The machine sewers earn still more, as much in many cases as 20s. a week. The explanation of this is that, when work is cheapened, people want much more of it. When sewing can be done so easily, more sewing is put into garments, and the garments being cheapened, more are bought. At the same time a good deal of the sewing, and finishing, and fitting, cannot be done by machinery, and this furnishes plenty of employment for those who cannot work machines.

If masons were to employ machines for cutting stone, they would be benefited like the seamstresses, instead of being injured. The cost of cutting stone by hand is now so great that people cannot build many stone buildings, nor use stone to decorate brick buildings, unless they are wealthy people. Were the dressing of stone much cheapened by the aid of machinery, a great deal more stone would be used, and the masons, instead of labouring at the dull work of cutting flat surfaces, would find plenty of employ-ment in finishing, and carving, and setting the machine-shaped stones. I have not the least doubt that, in addition to those engaged in working the machines, there would in the end be more masons wanted after the general introduction of machines than before. With type-setters the same thing will happen, if they take betimes to the new type-composing machines. It is true that a man with the aid of a good machine can set types several times as fast as without. But though the wages paid for setting a certain number of types might thus be reduced, so many more books, pamphlets, newspapers, and documents of various kinds would be printed, that no want of employment could be felt. Much of the work, too, such as the justifying, correcting, making into pages, &c., cannot be done by machinery, or not profitably, so that there would be plenty of work even for those who would not consent to work machines.

The fact is that **wages are increased by increasing the produce of labour, not by decreasing the produce.** The wages of the whole working population consist of the total produce remaining after the subtraction of rent, interest, and taxes. People get high wages in Lancashire because they use spinning machinery, which can do an immense quantity of work compared with the number of hands employed. If they refused to use machinery, they would have to spin cotton by hand like the poor inhabitants of Cashmere. Were there no machinery of any kind in England we should, nearly all of us, be as poor as the agricultural labourers of Wiltshire lately were.

People lose sight of the fact that **we do not work for the sake of working, but for the sake of what we produce by working.** The work itself is the disagreeable price paid for the wages earned, and these wages consist of the greater part of the value of the goods produced. It is absurd to suppose that people can become richer by having less riches. To become richer we must make more riches, and the object of every workman should be not to make work, but to make goods as rapidly and abundantly as possible.

56. **Piece-Work.** Some trades unions endeavour to prevent their members from earning wages by piece work, that is, by payment for the quantity of work done, instead of payment for the time spent in doing it. If a man is paid tenpence an hour, whether he work quickly or slowly, it is evidently for his interest to work slowly rather than quickly, provided that he be not so lazy as to run a risk of being discharged. It is a well known fact that men employed on piece-work do much more work in the same time than those employed on time jobs, and it is altogether better that they should be paid by the piece when the work done can be exactly measured and paid for. The men earn better wages because they are incited to do so much more, and they earn it more fairly, as a general rule. Trades-unions, however, sometimes object to piece-work, the reason given being that it makes the men work too hard, and thus injures their health. But this is an absurd reason; for men must generally be supposed capable of taking care of their own health. There are many trades and professions in which people are practically paid by the piece, but it is not found necessary to have trades-unions to keep them from killing themselves. There is more fear that people will work too little rather than too much.

The real objection which trades-unionists feel to piece-work is that it gets the work done quickly, and thus tends, as they think, to take employment away from other men. But, as I have already explained, men do not work for the sake of working, but for the sake of what they produce, and the more men in general produce, the higher wages in general will be. Trades-unionists put forward their views on the ground of unselfishness. They would say that it is selfish of Tom to work so as to take away employment from Dick and Harry; but they overlook the thousands of Toms, Dicks, and Harrys in other employments who get small wages indeed, and who are perhaps prevented by their rules from earning more. If the nation as a whole is to be wealthy and happy, we must each of us work to the best of our powers, producing the wealth which we can best produce, and not grudging others a greater success, it Providence has given them superior powers. People can seldom produce wealth for themselves without spreading a greater benefit over society in general, by cheapening commodities and lightening toil.

57. **The Fallacy of Equality.** Workmen often show a dislike to allowing one man to earn more than another in the same shop, and at the same kind of work. This feeling is partly due to the mistaken notion that in doing more work than others he takes employment from them. It partly, however, arises from a dislike to see one man better off than his mates. This feeling is not confined to workmen. Any one who reflects upon the state of society must regret that the few are so rich, and the many so poor. It might seem that the laws must be wrong which allow such differences to exist. It is needful to reflect, therefore, that such differences of wealth are not for the most part produced by the laws. All men, it has been said, are born free and equal; it is difficult to see how they can be born free, when, for many years after birth, they are helpless and dependent on their parents, and are properly under their governance. No doubt they ought to become free when grown up, but then they are seldom equal. One youth is stout, healthy and energetic; another puny and weak; one bright and intelligent; another dull and slow. Over these differences of body and mind the laws have no power. An Act of Parliament cannot make a weak frame strong. It follows that in after life some men must be capable of earning more than others. Out of every thousand men and women, too, there will be a few who are distinguished by remarkable talents or inventive genius. One man by patient labour and

great sagacity invents a sewing machine, a telegraph, or a telephone, and he thus confers the greatest possible advantage upon other men for centuries after.

It is obviously to the advantage of everybody that those who are capable of benefiting society should be encouraged to do so by giving them all the reward possible, by patents, copyright, and the laws of property generally. To prevent or discourage a clever man in doing the best work he can, is certainly no benefit to other men. It tends to level all down to a low standard, and to retard progress altogether. Every man, on the contrary, who is incited to work, and study, and invent to the utmost of his powers, not only earns welfare for himself, but confers welfare upon other people. He shows how wealth may be created abundantly, and how toil may be lessened. What is true of great ability and great inventions is true, also, of the smallest differences of power or the slightest improvements. If one bricklayer's labourer can carry up more bricks than another, why should he be prevented from doing it? The ability is his property, and it is for the benefit of all that he should be allowed to use it. If he finds a better way of carrying bricks, of course it should be adopted in preference to worse ways. The purpose of carrying bricks is to get them carried and benefit those who want houses. Everything which makes it difficult and expensive to build houses, causes people to be lodged worse than they otherwise would be. We can only get things made well and cheaply if every man does his best, and is incited to do so by gaining the reward of his excellence.

Every man then should not only be allowed, but should be encouraged to do and to earn all that he can ; we must then allow the greatest inequalities of wealth ; for a man who has once begun to grow rich, acquires capital, and experience, and means which enable him to earn more and more. Moreover, it is altogether false to suppose that, as a general rule, he does this by taking wealth from other people. On the contrary, by accumulating capital, by building mills, warehouses, railways, docks, and by skilfully organising trades, he often enables thousands of men to produce wealth, and to earn wages to an extent before impossible. The profits of a capitalist are usually but a small fraction of what he pays in wages, and he cannot become rich without assisting many workmen to increase the value of their labour and to earn a comfortable subsistence.

CHAPTER IX.

CO-OPERATION, &c.

58. Arbitration. We have now considered at some length the evils arising from the present separation of interests between the employed and their employers. The next thing is to discuss the various attempts which have been made to remedy these evils, and to bring labour and capital into harmony with each other. In the first place, many people think that when any dispute takes place, arbitrators or judges should be appointed to hear all that can be said on both sides of the question, and then decide what the rate of wages is to be for some time to come.

No doubt a good deal may be said in favour of such a course, but it is nevertheless inconsistent with the principles of free labour and free trade. If the judges are to be real arbitrators, they must have power to compel obedience to their decision, so that they will destroy the liberty of the workman to work or not as he likes, and of the capitalist to deal freely with his own capital, and sell goods at whatever price suits the state of the market. If wages are to be arbitrarily settled in this way, there is no reason why the same thing should not be done with the prices of corn, iron, cotton, and other goods. But legislators have long since discovered the absurdity of attempting

to fix prices by law. These prices depend entirely
upon supply and demand, and no one is really able to
decide with certainty what will be the conditions of
supply and demand a month or two hence. Government might almost as wisely legislate about the
weather we are to have next summer as about the
state of trade, which much depends upon the weather,
or upon wars and accidents of various kinds, which
no one can foresee. It is impossible, then, to fix
prices and wages beforehand by any kind of law or
compulsory decision. The matter is one of bargain,
of buying and selling, and the employer must be at
liberty to buy the labour required at the lowest price
at which he can get it, and the labourers to sell their
labour at the highest price they can get, both subject
of course to the legal notice of a week or fortnight.

59. **Conciliation.** Though the compulsory fixing
of wages is evidently objectionable, much good may
be done by **conciliators,** who are men chosen to
conduct a friendly discussion of the matters in dispute.
The business is arranged in various ways ; sometimes
three or more delegates of the workmen meet an
equal number of delegates from the masters, who
place before the meeting such information as they
think proper to give, and then endeavour to come to
terms. In other cases the delegates lay their respective
views before a man of sound and impartial judgment,
who then endeavours to suggest terms to which both
sides can accede. If the two parties previously engage
that they will accept the decision of this conciliator or
umpire, the arrangement differs little from arbitration,
except that there is no legal power to compel com-
pliance with the decision. Discredit has been thrown
upon this form of conciliation by the fact that the
workmen have in several instances refused to abide by
the award of the umpire when given against them, and
of course it cannot be expected that masters will
accept adverse decisions as binding under such circumstances. Thus I am led to think that the con-

ciliator should not attempt to be a judge; he should be merely an impartial friend of both sides, trying to remove misapprehension and hostile feelings, enlightening each party as to the views and reasons and demands of the other—acting, in short, as a go-between, and smoothing down the business as oil eases the movement of a machine. The final settlement must take the form of a voluntary bargain directly between the employers and employed, which will only have compulsory effect during the week or fortnight for which workmen usually enter into a legal agreement. Conciliation may in this way do much good, but it cannot remove the causes of difference—it cannot make the men feel that their interest is one with the interest of their employers.

60. **Co-operation.** Among the measures proposed for improving the position of workmen, the best is co-operation, if we understand by this name **the uniting together of capital and labour.** The name co-operation is used indeed with various meanings, and some of the arrangements called by it have really nothing to do with what we are now considering. **To co-operate means to work together** (Latin, *con*, together, and *operor*, to work). About thirty-five years ago some workmen of Rochdale, noticing the great profits made by shopkeepers in retail trade, resolved to work together by buying their own supplies wholesale, and distributing them amongst the members of the society which they established. They called this **a co-operative society,** and a great number of so-called co-operative stores have since been established. Most of these are nothing but shops belonging to a society of purchasers, who agree to buy at the store and divide the profits. They have on the whole done a great deal of good by leading many men to save money and to take an interest in the management of affairs. The stores are also useful, because they compete with shopkeepers, and induce them to lower their prices and to treat their customers better. We

frequently hear now of shops selling goods at **co-operative prices.**

But such co-operative societies have little or nothing to do with the subject of capital and labour. Commonly these stores are conducted less upon the true co-operative principle than ordinary shops. A shop is usually managed by the owner or by a man who has a large interest in its success, and has the best reasons for taking trouble. Co-operative stores, on the contrary, are often managed by men who are paid by salary or wages only, and have nothing to do with the profits and the capital of the concern.

Real co-operation consists in making all those who work share in the profits. At present a workman sells his labour for the best price he can get, and has nothing further to do with the results. If he does his work well, his master gets the benefit, and if he works badly his master is injured. It is true that he must not be very lazy or negligent for fear of being discharged; but if he takes care to be moderately careful and active, it is all that he need do for his own interests. No doubt it would be a good thing to reward the more active workmen with higher wages, and a wise employer endeavours to do this when he can, and to put the best workmen into the best places. But the trades-unions usually prevent it as far as they can, by insisting that men doing the same kind of work in the same place shall be paid alike. Moreover, as we have seen, many men are under the mistaken belief that if they work hard they decrease the demand for employment, and tend to take away the bread from their fellow-men. Thus it is not uncommon for workmen to study **how not to do the work too quickly,** instead of striving to make the most goods in the least time with the least trouble. Workmen do not see that what they produce forms in the long run their wages, so that if all workmen could be incited to activity and carefulness, wages would rise in all trades.

61. Industrial Partnerships. The best way of reconciling labour and capital would be to give every workman a share in the profits of his factory when trade is so prosperous as to allow of it. Charles Babbage proposed, in the year 1832, that a part of the wages of every person employed should depend on the profits of the employers. In recent years this has been tried in several large works, especially in Messrs. Briggs' collieries, and in Messrs. Fox, Head & Co.'s iron-works. The arrangement generally made with the men was that the capitalists should first take enough of the profits to pay 10 per cent. interest on the capital, together with fair salaries for the managers as wages of superintendence, a sum to meet bad debts, the repairs and depreciation of the machinery, and all other ordinary causes of loss. Such profit as remained was then divided into two equal parts, one of which went to the employers, while the other was divided among the workpeople in proportion to the amounts of wages which they had received during the year. Many workmen under such a scheme found themselves at Christmas in possession of five or ten pounds, in addition to the ordinary wages of the trade received weekly during the year.

This kind of co-operation has been called **industrial partnership,** and, if it could be widely carried into effect, there would arise many advantages. The workmen, feeling that their Christmas bonuses depended upon the success of the works, would not favour idleness, and would have some inducement for preventing needless waste whether of time or materials. By degrees they would learn that **the best trades-union is a union with their employers.** Strikes and lock-outs would be for the most part a thing of the past, because, if wages were too low, the balance-sheet would prove the fact at the end of the year, and half the surplus would go to the workmen. To be free from the danger of strikes would be a very great advantage to the employers, and any portion of profits which they might seem to give up would be more than repaid by the increased care and activity of the workmen. The employers would continue to manage the business entirely according to their own judgment, and they need not make their affairs or accounts known to the men. All that is requisite is that skilful accountants should examine the books at the end of the year, and certify the amount of profits due to the men. If this plan were thoroughly carried out, the men would feel that they were really working for themselves as much as for their masters, and the troubles which at present exist would be nearly unknown.

There are great difficulties in the way of this kind of co-operation : most capitalists do not like it, because they needlessly fear to make known their profits to their men, and they do not understand the advantages which would arise from a better state of things. The workmen also do not like the arrangement, because the trades-unions oppose co-operation, fearing that it will overthrow their own power. Where the scheme has been tried, it has usually succeeded well, until the men, urged by their trades-unions, refused to go on with it. Thus are people, through prejudice and want of knowledge, made blind to the best interests of themselves and the country.

It is to be feared, then, that industrial partnerships will not make much progress just at present, so great is the dislike to them felt both by trades-unions and by prejudiced employers. Nevertheless, the arrangement is in accordance with the principles of political economy, and it will probably be widely adopted by some future generation. Already, indeed, many banks, mercantile firms, and public companies practically recognise the value of the principle, by giving bonuses or presents to their clerks at the end of a profitable year. A French railway company adopted this practice forty years ago, and as business falls more and more into the hands of companies whose profits are matters of general knowledge, there seems to be no reason whatever why the principle of industrial partnership should not be adopted. Somewhat the same principle is said to be carried into effect in the very extensive and successful newspaper business of Messrs. W. H. Smith & Son.

62. Joint-Stock Co-operation. Another mode of co-operation consists in working men saving up their wages until they have got small capitals, so that they can unite together and own the factories, machines, and materials with which they work. They then become their own capitalists and employers, and secure all the profit to themselves. Co-operative societies of this kind are simply Joint-Stock Companies, the shares of which are held by the men employed. Of course the shareholders must choose directors from among themselves, and they must also have managers to arrange the business. The managers and directors ought to be well paid for what they do, and have a considerable share of the profits, in order to make them interested in the success of the works, and therefore active and careful. Incompetent or negligent management will soon ruin the best business.

A great number of co-operative companies of this kind have been formed in the last twenty years in England, France, America, and elsewhere; but most of them have failed from want of good direction. The working-men shareholders do not generally understand what a great deal of skill and judgment is required in the conduct of a business; they are accustomed to see work going on as if it went of its own accord, but they do not see the constant anxiety and the careful calculation which is requisite to make the work profitable. Hence they usually fail to secure good managers, and they do not sufficiently trust those whom they appoint. Moreover, many of the so-called co-operative companies are not really co-operative; they frequently employ men who are neither shareholders nor receivers of a share of profits, and they pay their

8

managers by a small fixed salary. **Such co-operative societies are badly-managed joint-stock
companies, and cannot be expected to succeed well.**

Another difficulty with such companies is, that they
rarely have enough capital, and, when bad trade
comes, they are unable to bear the losses which will
sometimes occur for several years in succession. They
can borrow money by the mortgage of the buildings
and machinery belonging to the company, and this is
usually done; but no banker will give credit to such
companies without the security of fixed property.
Thus they frequently fail when bad trade comes, and
those who buy up their property cheaply reap advantage. It is to be hoped that at a future time all
working-men will become capitalists on a small
scale, and when education and experience have been
acquired, co-operative factories of working-men may
succeed. At present it would be better to leave the
management of business in the hands of capitalists,
who are not only experienced and clever men, but
have the best reason to be careful and active, because
their fortunes depend upon success.

63. **Providence.** It is most deeply to be re-
gretted that the working-people of England will not,
for the most part, see the necessity of saving a portion
of their wages in order to have something to live upon
when trade is bad, or when ill-health and misfortune
come upon them. Too many working-men's families
spend all that is earned while trade is brisk, and when
employment fails they are as badly off as ever.
**There are several distinct reasons why every
man or woman should save up some property when possible:—**

(1) It forms a provision in case of ill-health, accident, want of employment, or other misfortune; it is also wanted for support in old age,
or for the helpless widow and orphans of a
workman who dies early.

(2) It yields interest, and adds to a workman's income.

(3) It enables a man to go into trade, to buy good tools, and to enjoy good credit in case he sees an opportunity of setting up business on his own account.

No man and no woman, who is in the prime of life and earning fair wages, should spend the whole. Even an unmarried person will generally reach a time of life when, through ill health, old age, or other unavoidable causes, it is no longer possible to get a living. By that time enough ought to have been saved to avoid the need of charity or the degradation of the poor-house. When there is a wife and young family, the need of saving is evidently greater still. Every great storm, colliery explosion, or other great accident leaves a number of helpless children to be brought up by a struggling widow, or to go on the parish. No doubt people may meet with disasters so unexpected and so great that they cannot be blamed for not providing against them. A man who is blinded, or crippled, or otherwise disabled in early life, is a proper object of charity, but there would be plenty of benevolent institutions to provide for such exceptional cases, if those who are more fortunate would provide properly for themselves.

It is often said that working men really cannot save out of the small wages they receive; the expenses of living are too great. We cannot deny that there are labourers, especially agricultural labourers in the South of England, whose wages will not do more than barely provide necessary food and clothing for their families. The weekly earnings of a family in some parts are not more than 12 or 15 shillings on the average of the year, and sometimes even less. Such people can hardly be expected to save. But this is not the case with the artisans and labourers in the manufacturing districts. They seldom earn less than a pound a week, and often two pounds. The boys and girls, and sometimes the mother of the family, also earn wages, so that when trade is brisk a family in Manchester or Leicester, or other manufacturing town, will get altogether £150 a year, or more. Some kinds of workmen, especially coal-hewers, and iron-puddlers, earn twice that amount in good years, and are in fact better paid than schoolmasters, ministers of religion, and upper clerks. It is idle to say that the better-paid working men cannot save, and though we cannot make any strict rule, it is probable that **all who earn more than a pound (five dollars, or 25 francs) a week, might save something.**

It is easy to prove this assertion by the fact that when a strike occurs, men voluntarily live on a half, or a third of their ordinary wages. Sometimes they will live for three or four months on 12 or 15 shillings a week, which is paid for their support by their trades-union, or by other unions, which subscribe money to assist them. It is quite common for workmen to pay **levies,** that is, almost compulsory subscriptions of a shilling or more a week, to be spent by other workmen who are **playing,** as it is called, during a long strike. Nobody wishes working people to live on the half of their wages, but **if, for the purpose of carrying on struggles against their employers, they can spare these levies, it is evident that they could spare them for the purpose of saving.** Then, again, we know that the money spent on drink is enormous in amount; in this country it is about £140,000,000 a year, or about four pounds a year for every man, woman, and child. To say the least, half of this might be saved, with the greatest advantage to the health and morals of the savers, and thus the working classes would be able to lay by an annual sum not much less than the revenue of the nation.

CHAPTER X.

TENURE OF LAND.

64. We have sufficiently considered the difficulties which exist regarding **Labour** and **Capital,** two of the requisites of production, and we will now turn to another part of political economy, and inquire into the way in which **Land,** the third requisite, is supplied.

In different countries land is held in very different ways. It is a matter of custom, and in the course of time customs slowly change. The way in which farms are owned and managed in England at the present time is no indication of the way land is held in France, or Norway, or Russia, or even the United States; nor is it the same as the way in which farms were owned in England some centuries ago. What is fitting to one place and state of society will not necessarily be fitting in other circumstances. We have to consider the various ways in which the requisites of production, land, labour, and capital, are brought together; sometimes they are all furnished by the same person; sometimes by separate persons.

In the condition of **slavery,** for instance, as it existed in the Southern States of North America, the owner of an estate owned the land, labour, and capital, all at once. Strictly speaking a slave is not a labourer, because he cannot sell his labour at his own price, and work or not as he likes. He is more in the position of the horse which drags the plough, a mere beast of burden. Just as a farmer owns his horses, and cows, and pigs, as part of his capital, so a slave-owner treats his slaves as part of his capital. Slave-labour being given unwillingly, and without hope of reward, is usually badly given, and is wasteful; but there is hardly any need to consider whether slavery is good or bad in an economical point of view, because it is altogether condemned from a moral point of view. We may show the way the requisites of production are furnished in **slavery** by the following diagram—

Slave-Owner.

Land.   Labour.   Capital.

In a very large part of the world, again, the government takes the place of land-owners, and collects the rent by means of tax-gatherers. The farming is done by poor peasants, who find the capital, so far as there is any, and also do the work. Thus, we have the arrangement—

Government.   Peasant.

Land.   Capital.   Labour.

This system is called **Ryot Tenure**, and it exists at the present day in Turkey, Egypt, Persia, and many eastern countries; also in a somewhat altered form in British India. After slavery, it is the worst of all systems, because the Government can fix the rent at what it likes, and it is difficult to distinguish between rent and taxes. When their crops fail the ryot peasants are unable to pay the tax-gatherers, and they get into debt and become quite helpless.

65. **Peasant Proprietorship.** One of the best modes of holding land, when it can exist, is that known as peasant proprietorship, because the owner of the land is the peasant himself, who labours with his own arms, and finds the capital also. In this system, as in slavery, all the requisites of production are in the same hands; thus—

Peasant.

Land.   Labour.   Capital.

But in every other respect this system is the opposite of slavery. Its advantages are evident; the labourer being the owner of the farm and of all upon it, is an independent man, who has every inducement to work hard, and to increase his savings. Every little improvement which he can make in his farm is so much added to his wealth, and that of his family after him. There is what is called the **magic of property.** The feeling that he is working entirely for his own and his family's benefit **almost magically increases his inclination to work.** In newly-settled countries, such as the Western Territories of the United States, and Canada, or the colonies of Australia, and the Cape, this mode of holding land seems to be suitable, because the land is there very cheap, and crops can be raised with little capital. In such countries there is no need of expensive manures, elaborate machinery, and the cost of draining and improving land.

The objection to peasant proprietorship is, that he who does the labour of a farm with his own hands, must usually be a poor and unskilful person. If he were rich he would probably prefer to buy up the labour of other men, and become a capitalist farmer; if he were a really skilful farmer, it would be a pity to waste his skill upon a small farm, when, with more division of labour, he might profitably direct and manage a large one. Being poor, his capital will be mostly absorbed in building his cottage and barns, and in paying the small price of his land; he will have little left to make improvements, or to buy good labour-saving implements, and good stock, such as well-bred horses, cows, and pigs. Thus, unless his land be new and very fertile, he will not get a large return for his labour. Owing to the magic of property, he may work very hard, and during long hours, but he will not work in an economical way, and therefore will remain poor in spite of his severe exertions. The peasant proprietors who still exist in Switzerland, Belgium, Norway, Sweden, and some other parts of Europe, work almost day and night during the summer, and they are very careful and saving; yet they seldom grow rich, or get more than a bare living out of the soil.

Too frequently the peasant proprietor, if he is not very provident, runs short of money after one or two bad seasons. He will then be tempted to borrow money, to sell his timber, and other produce before it is ready for the market, and thus run in debt. When his farm has increased in value and would bring some rent, he will very likely mortgage it, that is, give it by a legal deed as security for his debts. The mortgagee or lender of the money then becomes part-owner of the land and capital, so that the arrangement tends to take this form—

Money-Lender.		Peasant.	
Land.	Capital.	Capital.	Labour.

66. Tenure of Land in England. As agriculture becomes more a science, farming will require greater skill, and larger capital, and the English mode of land tenure will probably spread. In this system there is the greatest division of labour, and different ranks of people have shares in the business, somewhat as follows :—

Proprietor.		Farmer.		Labourer.
Land.	Capital.	Capital.	Labour.	Labour.

The land is usually owned by some rich man, who likes to have large estates, but does not wish to have the trouble of farming. In respect of the land only he is a **proprietor of a natural agent,** and the rent he receives is true rent; but there will usually be buildings, roads, fences, drains, and other improvements, of which he is also owner; in respect of these he is a capitalist, and the return he receives is interest. The farmer is a man of knowledge and skill, with considerable capital; he hires the land and its improvements from the proprietor, and stocks it with cattle, carts, improved implements of all kinds, and then employs day-labourers to do the manual work, labouring himself in superintendence, in keeping accounts, buying and selling, &c. The labourer, generally speaking, is nothing but a labourer; he lives in a cottage hired probably from the farmer or proprietor, and he has little motive for working harder than he is made to do, because the advantage goes to his employer.

In this arrangement there are great advantages, and also great disadvantages. The farmer, being an intelligent man, acquainted with agricultural science, and furnished with plenty of capital, can adopt all the latest inventions, and raise the largest possible produce from the land and labour. It is also advantageous that the farmer does not own the land and fixed capital, because this leaves all his own capital free to provide more expensive implements and manures, and finer kinds of cattle. It is also a good thing that farms will, on this system, be large, so that there will be considerable division of labour, almost as in a factory; thus there will arise some of the advantages which were described as belonging to the Division of Labour (Sections 25—29).

The disadvantages of the English mode of farming are also great, especially as regards the labourers, the most numerous class. They have none of the independence of peasant proprietors, and, when dismissed, or too old to work, have probably to go to the workhouse. Their wages have hitherto been very low, and saving was not possible. But this state of things is partly due to the bad Poor Laws which used to exist in England, and to the excessive numbers of poor, ignorant labourers. After a time, when the poor laws are improved, when labourers become more educated, and are employed, like factory hands, to work machines, there is no reason why they should not get good wages, and become independent, like artisans.

In the English system, a great deal depends upon the nature of the agreement between the land-owner and the capitalist farmer. Many large land-owners in England refuse to let their land for long periods

They like to have farmers who are **tenants at will,**
and can be turned off their farms at a year's notice,
and deprived of the value of all the improvements
they have made, if they offend the great land-owner.
It is easy to understand this ; the land-owners wish to
be lords, and to rule affairs in their own neighbour-
hood, as if they were little kings.   This sort of thing
is called **territorial influence,** and men who have
become rich by making iron or cotton goods, often
buy estates at a high price, in order to enjoy the
pleasure of feeling like lords.   The rural parts of
England, Scotland, and Ireland are still, in fact, under
the feudal system.

In a Primer like this we have to look at the matter
as regards political economy only, and in this respect
the arrangement described is bad.   Tenants at will
have no inducement to improve their farms, because
this would tempt the land-owner to turn them out, or
to raise the rent.   It is generally understood, indeed,
that a land-owner will not use his power, so that many
farmers act as if they were sure of holding their farms ;
if turned out after all, they are practically robbed of
their capital ; and, in any case, they cannot possibly
feel the independence which every man ought to
enjoy.   We must always remember that the laws
should be made not for the benefit of any one class,
but for the benefit of the whole country.   The laws
concerning landlord and tenant have, however, been
made by landlords, and are more fitted to promote
their enjoyment than to improve agriculture.

There are two modes of remedying the unfortunate
state of land tenure in this country, namely :—
    (1) By a system of long leases.
    (2) By tenant right.

67. Leasehold Tenure. A lease is a formal
agreement to let land or houses to a tenant for a certain
number of years at a fixed rent, and with various conditions, which are carefully stated, to prevent mis-
understanding.   When land is taken by a farmer

under a lease for thirty years or more, it becomes almost like his own property, because, in the earlier part of his term, he can make great improvements with the aid of his capital, and yet be sure of getting the value back before the lease comes to an end. In the eastern parts of England and Scotland, where the farms are largest and best managed, these long leases are the usual mode of letting land. It is certainly one of the best arrangements for promoting good farming, and it has few disadvantages, except that the farmer will not make improvements towards the end of his lease.

68. **Tenant Right.** Another good arrangement is tenant right, which consists in **giving the tenant a right to claim the value of any unexhausted improvements,** which he may have made in his farm, if he be turned out of it. A farmer can prove without difficulty how much he has spent in building barns, stables, piggeries, &c., in draining the lands, making roads and fences, or in putting lime and costly manures into the soil. Those who are experienced in farming can form a good judgment how long each improvement will continue profitable, so as to calculate how much the tenant loses if he be turned away. Thus a good estimate may be formed as to the sum which the tenant should receive as compensation, and the landlord, if he chooses to dismiss the tenant, should be obliged to pay this compensation. He will get it back by charging a higher rent to the next tenant.

Tenant right, though unknown in most parts of England, is not at all a new system; it has existed for a long time in the north of Ireland, where it is called the **Ulster tenant right.** A new tenant there pays the old tenant a considerable sum of money for the privilege of getting a good farm with various improvements, and the land-owner is practically prevented from turning out a good tenant at his mere will. In Yorkshire also it has been the custom to compensate an outgoing tenant, and there is no good reason why the custom should not be made into a legal right, and extended over the whole country. Mr. Gladstone's Irish Land Act has already established a somewhat similar system throughout Ireland. If the land is to be used for its proper purposes, and not merely for the amusement and pride of a few landlords, **every owner of land who lets it should be obliged either to give a long lease, say of thirty or fifty years, or else to pay the compensation fixed by a jury** after taking evidence from those skilled in valuing farms. It should be made illegal to let land on any other terms.

69. The Cause of Rent. It is very important to understand exactly how rent arises, for without knowing this it is impossible to see why a landlord should be allowed to come and take away a considerable part of what is produced, without taking any other trouble in the matter. But the fact is that we cannot do away with rents : they must go to some one or other, and the only real question which can arise is whether there shall be many landlords receiving small rents or few landlords with great rent-rolls.

Rent arises from the fact that different pieces of land are not equally fertile, that is, they do not yield the same quantities of produce for the same quantities of labour. This may arise from the soil being different, or from one piece of land getting more sun and moisture than another. If the earth had a perfectly smooth surface the same everywhere, and if it were all tilled and cultivated in exactly the same way, there would be no such thing as rent. But the earth's surface, as we know, has hills and valleys : there are flats of rich soil in one place, and wastes of dry sand and stones in other places. Now, where the soil is good and favourably situated for growing corn, or other produce, the owner of such land must get more, in return for his labour, than if he possessed a bad piece of land. Even then, if everybody owned the farm which he cultivates, those who owned the better pieces would get rent, because they would get more produce. Thus, after allowing the same wages to all, there would remain something in addition to the lucky owners of the better land. If, instead of working on this good land themselves, they let it to other workmen, they will be able to get a rent depending on the richness and the other advantages of the land.

Now there can be little difficulty in seeing how the amount of rent of land is governed. That land will pay no rent at all which only gives produce enough to pay the wages of the labourers who work upon it, together with the interest of any capital which they require. The rent of better land will then consist of the surplus of its produce over that of the poorest cultivated land, after allowance has been made for the greater or less amount of labour and capital expended on it. Or we may look at the matter in this way: The price of corn is decided by the cost of producing it on land which just pays the expenses of cultivation, because when more corn is needed, it is from such land we must procure it, the better land having been long since occupied. But corn of the same quality sells at the same price whatever be its cost of production; hence the rent of more fertile land will be the excess of the price of its produce over that of land which only just pays the cultivator and leaves no rent.

CHAPTER XI.

EXCHANGE.

70. **How Exchange Arises.** One of the most important ways in which we can increase wealth consists in exchange—in **giving what we do not want in return for what we do want.** Wealth, as we have seen, is anything which is actually useful to us, because we have not enough already, and which can be transferred to another person. But when our want of any kind of commodity is satisfied, we want no more of that, but we do want other kinds

of commodity. The result is that exchange constantly produces a **gain of utility.** Some people have objected that there can be no good in exchange, because that which is given equals in value that which · is received. Others have said that, if one party gains, it must evidently be by robbing the other party. According to this view, trade would consist in trying to beggar your neighbour. That which is given does really equal in value that which is received, but it does not equal it in utility, and to increase utility is the purpose of all production and all commerce. We do not pay for things in proportion to their usefulness, or else air and water would be the most costly of all' things. A good-sized loaf may be bought for four-pence or sixpence, although bread is the staff of life. Before attempting to understand this apparent paradox, we must settle exactly what we mean by value.

71. **What is Value?** In exchanging some goods for other goods, there arises the question, How much of one kind shall be given for so much of the other ? Some things are said to be **valuable,** as in the case of a gold watch or a diamond ring, because in exchange for them we can get a great quantity of other articles. Ashes are of little or no value, because we cannot get anything in exchange for them. Now this word **value** is a very difficult one, and is employed to mean different things. We may say that quinine is valuable for curing fevers, that iron is valuable for improving the blood, or that water is valuable for putting out fires. Here we do not mean valuable in exchange, for quinine would cure fevers just as well if it cost a penny an ounce instead of some ten shillings. Water, if we can get it at the right time, puts out a fire whether it costs much or little or nothing. It is clear, then, that by valuable we often mean **valuable in use.** The words value and valuable are in fact **ambiguous.** (See Logic Primer, pp. 22-26, on The Correct Use of Words.) **There is value in use and value in exchange, and many things**

which would be commonly said to have little value in exchange have much value in use. But of these meanings, "value in use" is nothing but the **utility** of a thing to us, that is, the utility of all such portions of it as we can actually employ. Thus, the value in use of water means the utility of the water that we drink, or wash in, or cook with, or water the roads with, and this utility is very great. But of course it cannot mean the utility of water which is not useful to us, but on the contrary hurtful, as in the case of floods, damp houses, wet mines, and so forth.

We may now see how true was the remark of Genovesi, the Italian economist, that "**Exchange consists in giving the superfluous for the necessary**," or, as I should prefer to say, **the comparatively superfluous for the comparatively necessary.** He who has more than enough of one article has already enjoyed all the good which that article can do to him, but he probably needs supplies of other articles. The exchange, like an act of mercy, blesses both him who gives and him who receives, because what each receives in exchange is much wanted and has high utility. In England, for instance, we possess a great deal of coal, and France produces plenty of good wine. We could have little or no wine in England unless we got it from France or some foreign country, and France also is much in want of coal. It is obvious that there is a great gain of utility if we give some of our comparatively superfluous coal in exchange for some of the abundant wine of France.

It has been objected to commerce that it is **sterile** and produces no new goods. There exist neither more nor less coal and wine after they are exchanged than before. But in political economy we treat of utility and wealth; the question is whether things are usefully consumed or not. Now that which is not wealth if it were consumed by one person, becomes wealth when handed over to another person for consumpti n. **Though exchange cannot create the** material of wealth, it creates wealth because it gives utility to the material.

72. **Value means Proportion in Exchange.** When we speak of the value of a thing in exchange, we mean how much of some other thing we can get for it. This of course will depend upon the nature of that other thing. Obviously, I can get for a shilling much more potatoes than bread, and bread than beef, and beef than essence of beef. Therefore, when we speak of the value of a thing, we ought always to say what it is to be valued by. **The word value only means that so much of one thing is given for so much of the other,** and it is the **proportion** of these quantities (Latin *proportio*, from *pro*, in comparison with, and *portio*, share), which measures the values of the thing. A ton of pig-iron can usually be got for a quarter of corn ; here the proportion is one to one. To get a ton of copper, we should probably have to give thirty quarters of corn ; here the proportion is that of one to thirty. There cannot be such a thing as value in exchange, unless there be proportion —so much of one commodity for so much of another.

Usually, indeed, we measure the values of things by their **prices.** The **price is the quantity of money which we give for a thing ;** in this case the proportion is between the quantity of money and the quantity of goods we get for it, as when we give sixty shillings for ten yards of carpet. We shall learn later on that money is a kind of commodity, which has utility and value like other commodities. But there is great convenience in always thinking and speaking of values in money, because we can then readily compare the value of one thing with that of any other. If a pound of potatoes costs one penny, a pound of bread threepence, and a pound of beef ninepence, we can see at once that a pound of beef is of the same value as three pounds of bread and nine pounds of potatoes, and we can judge how much of each to use.

73. Laws of Supply and Demand. In the next place, we must try to understand how the values of things are governed, and made to change from time to time. The principal laws which govern values are called **the laws of supply and demand,** and they are very important indeed. **Supply** means the quantity of any goods which people are willing to give in exchange at a certain value, and **demand** means similarly the quantity of goods which people are willing to take in exchange; but, before a person can judge how much he wishes to buy of a particular kind of goods, he must know its price, that is, its proportion in exchange for money. If bread, instead of being threepence per pound, becomes fourpence, a poor person would perhaps decide to take less bread, and to buy more potatoes. If beef, instead of being ninepence, should rise to a shilling, or fourteenpence a pound, some people would refuse to buy it altogether, and others would buy less than before. The supply of things varies similarly; if the price of meat rises high, farmers who own cattle bring them to market, in order to get a good profit by selling them; if the price falls low, they keep their cattle to sell at another time.

The Laws of Supply and Demand may be thus stated: a rise of price tends to produce a greater supply and a less demand; a fall of price tends to produce a less supply and a greater demand. Conversely, an increase of supply or a decrease of demand tends to lower price, and a decrease of supply or an increase of demand to raise price.

These laws are so important that I will state them over again, in the form of a table :—

Price.	Supply.	Demand.
Higher.	Greater.	Less.
Lower.	Less.	Greater.

We can now understand how the price of any kind of goods is decided. The price must be such that the quantity demanded at any time is equal to the quantity supplied. If those who want goods at a certain price, cannot get them, they will have to offer a higher price, so that they may induce other people to sell. The higher the price the greater the supply, as we have seen; moreover, if some people in a market are offering a higher price, it soon becomes known to other dealers. When a farmer's wife carries a basket of butter to sell at the Butter Cross in the neighbouring market town, she soon learns whether the supply is greater or less than usual. If the purchasers are few and slow in buying, she begins to fear that she may have to carry her butter back unsold, and go without the crockery and calico and other things which she intended to buy with the money. Then she begins to ask a penny or twopence a pound less, and the other sellers of butter are obliged to lower their prices also, since no one would buy butter from one woman at 1s. 6d., if he could get it as good from the next person at 1s. 4d. But, if few people bring butter to market, or if there are many purchasers with money in their pockets, the scene is quite changed. Those who have brought butter, find that they will have no difficulty in selling all they have; it is the purchasers who now become anxious to buy before all is gone, and their eagerness soon shows the sellers that they may ask higher prices. It is by this **higgling of the market,** by sellers asking the highest price they think they can get, and buyers trying to buy at the lowest price which they think will be taken—that the market price of any commodity is settled.

The market price will be such that the demand at that price will equal the supply at that price. The quantity of butter or any other commodity that is sold must equal what is bought, because it is not sold until it is bought; but the price will settle itself accordingly.

74. How Value depends upon Labour. We now come to the great question whether value is produced by labour, or how it is connected with labour. Some economists, observing that, when a thing like gold is very valuable, men spend a great deal of labour in getting it, have said that **the labour spent upon it is the cause of the high value.** **This is quite wrong;** for if it were true, anything, upon which great labour has been spent, ought to be very valuable; everybody knows that such is not the case. Great labour may be expended in writing, printing, and binding a book; but, if nobody wants the book, it is valueless, except as waste paper. A vast amount of labour was spent on building the Thames Tunnel, but, as few people wished to go through it, the tunnel was of small value, until it was required for a railway. Thus it is quite certain that we cannot make a thing valuable by simply labouring at it; we must labour in such a way as to make the thing useful.

On the other hand, substances may be very valuable which have cost little or no labour. When a shepherd in Australia happens to pick up a nugget of gold on the mountain side, it takes no labour worth mentioning to pick it up, yet the gold is just as valuable in proportion to its weight as any other gold. Some gold mines produce a great quantity of gold : others which have cost quite as much to sink, produce little ; nevertheless the gold out of the one mine is sold at the same price in proportion to its weight and fineness as that out of the other mine. **Thus it is quite certain that labour is not the cause of value.** Gold is valuable because a great many people want more gold than they have already got, and whenever a thing is valuable it is because somebody wants it.

But we may look at this matter in another way. If it were possible to get a valuable thing like gold with little labour, many people would become gold miners. Much gold would then be produced; if this were wanted as much as what was already in use, it would be as valuable. But no one wants an unlimited quantity of any substance. Wealth, as we saw, must be limited in supply; if gold became as plentiful as lead or iron, it could not possibly remain as valuable as it is now. People would have far more than they could employ for ornaments, watches, gilding and so forth; there would be a large surplus to be used in making pots and pans, for which it is less needed. Now we can see through the whole subject of value. When much of a substance can usually be produced with little labour, the substance becomes so plentiful that people are satisfied with the supplies of it which they have; they do not want more, or at least do not want it so urgently. It follows that they are unwilling to give much wealth for it. Thus the labour spent upon producing a commodity does not affect the value of that commodity, unless it alters the quantity of it which people can get, and thus makes a further supply of the commodity more or less useful than before.

75. **Why Pearls are valuable.** To make this still more plain, let us endeavour to answer this difficult question, "Do men dive for pearls because pearls fetch a high price, or do pearls fetch a high price because men must dive in order to get them?" Pearl-diving is a very dangerous and laborious kind of work. The divers have to jump into the deep sea with heavy weights to carry them down, and they must hold their breath a long time while they are engaged in collecting the oyster shells at the bottom. The number of good pearls which they generally get is small compared with the great toil of getting them. It follows that, on the average, they must receive a high price for what they do find, otherwise they would not have adequate wages for such work. But this alone is not a sufficient reason for the pearls being so valuable, otherwise the mother of pearl shells, in which the pearls are found, and brought up, would be as valuable as the pearls. But mother of pearl is

a very cheap substance. Again, if it were merely a question of labour, a diver might go down anywhere, and, bringing up the first stone or shell he found, insist on selling it for a high price, because he had dived for it. The truth is, that pearls are valuable because there are many ladies who have not got pearl necklaces, and who would like to have them ; and those who have some pearls would like to get more and finer ones. In short, then, pearls are valuable because they are useful to ladies who want more pearl ornaments : they are thus useful because the ladies have not hitherto been able to get as many as they would like ; and they have not been able to get many, because it is so difficult to fish them up from the bottom of the sea. Here we have the whole theory of value and labour. **The labour which is required to get more of a commodity governs the supply of it ; the supply determines whether people do or do not want more of it eagerly ; and this eagerness of want or demand governs value.**

CHAPTER XII.

MONEY.

76. **Barter.** When exchanges are made by giving one ordinary commodity for another, as a sack of corn for a side of bacon, or a book for a telescope, we are said to **barter** them. The operation is also called **truck** (French, *troc*, barter). Among uncivilised races trade is still carried on in this way ; a traveller going into the interior of South Africa takes a stock of beads, knives, pieces of iron, looking-glasses, &c., in order that he may always have something which the natives will like to receive in exchange for food or services. People still occasionally barter things in England, or the United States, but this is seldom done, owing to the trouble which it gives.

If, for instance, I want a telescope, in exchange for

a book, I shall probably have to make many inquiries, and to wait a long time before I meet with a person who has a telescope to spare, and who is also willing to take my book in exchange. It is very unlikely that he who has a telescope will just happen to want that particular book. A second difficulty is, that the book will probably not be worth just as much as the telescope, and neither more nor less. He who owns a valuable telescope cannot cut it up, and sell a part to one and a part to another ; this would destroy its value.

77. **Convenience of Money.** With the aid of money all the difficulties of barter disappear ; for **money consists of some commodity which all people in the country are willing to receive in exchange, and which can be divided into quantities of any amount.** Almost any commodity might be used as money in the absence of a better material. In agricultural countries corn was so used in former times. Every farmer had a stock of corn in his own granary, and if he wanted to buy a horse or cart, he took so many sacks of corn to his neighbour's granary in exchange. Now suppose that, with corn as money, a farmer wanted to part with a cart and get a plough instead; he need not inquire until he finds a person willing to receive a cart, and give a plough in exchange. It is sufficient if he find one farmer who will receive a cart and give corn, and any other farmer who will give a plough and receive corn. No difficulty arises, too, if the cart or plough are not of equal value ; for if the cart be the more valuable, then the farmer finally gets for it the plough together with enough corn to make up the difference. Money thus acts as a **medium of exchange** ; it is a go-between, or third term, and it facilitates exchange by dividing the act of barter into two acts, in this way—

Sale.   Purchase.

No doubt it turns one act of exchange into two; but the two are far more easy to manage than one, because they need not be made with the same person.

78. **Money as a Measure of Value.** When money is used in exchange, he who receives money is said **to sell goods,** and he who pays money is said **to buy or to purchase.** In each case there is an act of exchange, and sales and purchases are not really different in nature from acts of barter, except that one of the commodities given or received is employed for the purpose of arranging the exchange. Thus money may be called **current commodity,** because it is merchandise chosen **to run** about as a medium of exchange. Now, in every purchase or sale there must be some proportion between the quantity of the money, and the quantity of the other commodity. This proportion expresses the value of the one commodity as compared with the other. Value in exchange means nothing but this proportion, as was before explained (section 72). Now when money is used, the quantity of money given or received for a certain quantity of goods is called **the price of that goods,** so that the price is the value of goods = stated in money. But as money when once introduced is used in almost every act of exchange, a further great advantage arises. We are able to compare the value of any commodity with that of any other commodity. If we know how much copper may be had for so much lead; how much iron for so much steel; and so on with zinc and brass, bricks and timber, and so forth, it would not be possible to compare the value of copper with zinc, or iron with timber. But if we know that for one ounce of gold we can get 950 ounces of tin, 1,700 ounces of copper, 6,400 ounces of lead, and 16,000 ounces of wrought iron, then we learn without any trouble that for 1,700 ounces of copper we can get 16,000 ounces of iron, and so on. Thus gold or any other substance used as money serves as a **common measure of value;** it measures the value

of every other commodity, and thus enables us to compare the value of each commodity with that of every other.

This is an immense convenience. It leads every one to think and speak of the values of things in terms of a money known to everybody. All lists of values of goods are given as lists of prices and everybody understands these prices and can compare the prices in one list with those in another. Money may then be said to have two chief functions. It serves as

(1) **A medium of exchange.**

(2) **A common measure of value.**

But it is important to remember that, though money thus acts in a very useful and peculiar way, it never ceases to be a commodity. Its value is subject to the laws of supply and demand already stated (section 73); if the quantity of money increases, its value is likely to decrease, so that more money is given for the same commodity, and **vice versa.**

79. **What Money is made of.** As already remarked almost any commodity may be used as money, and in different ages all kinds of things such as wine, eggs, olive oil, rice, skins, tobacco, shells, nails, have actually been employed in buying and selling. But metals are found to serve much the best for several reasons, and gold and silver are better for the purpose than any of the other metals. The advantages of having gold and silver money are evident. Such metals are **portable,** because they are so valuable that a small weight of metal equals in value a great weight of corn or timber or other goods. Then they are **indestructible,** that is, they do not rot like timber, nor go bad like eggs, nor sour like wine; thus they can be kept for any length of time without losing their value. Another convenience is, that there is no difference in quality in the metal itself; pure gold is always the same as pure gold, and though it may be mixed with more or less base metal, yet we can assay or analyse the mixture, and ascertain

how much pure metal it contains. The metals are also **divisible;** they may be cut or coined into pieces, and yet the pieces taken together will be as valuable as before they were cut up. It is a further advantage of gold and silver that they are such beautiful, brilliant substances, and gold is also so heavy that it is difficult to make any counterfeit gold or silver; with a little experience and care, every one can tell whether he is getting real money or not— when the money is made of gold or silver. Finally, it is a great convenience that **these metals do not change in value rapidly.** A bad harvest makes corn twice as dear as before, and destructible things, like eggs, skins, &c., are always rising or falling in value. But gold and silver change slowly in value, because they last so long, and thus the new supply got in any one year is very little compared with the whole supply or stock of the metal. Nevertheless, **gold and silver, like all other commodities, are always changing in value more or less quickly.**

80. **Metallic Money.** Almost all the common metals—copper, iron, tin, lead, &c.—have been used to make money at one time or other, besides various mixtures, such as brass, pewter, and bronze. But copper, silver, and gold have been found far more suitable than any of the other metals. Copper, indeed, being comparatively low in value, is wanting in portability. It was formerly the only money of Sweden, and I have seen a piece of old Swedish money consisting of a plate of copper about two feet long and one foot broad. A merchant making payments in such money had to carry his money about in a wheel-

to use gold, silver, and bronze money according as each is convenient. **In the English system of money, gold is the standard money and the legal tender,** because no one can be obliged to receive a large sum of money in any other metal. If a person owes a hundred pounds, he cannot get rid of the debt without tendering or offering a hundred pieces of coined gold to his creditor. Silver coin is a legal tender only to the amount of forty shillings— that is, no creditor can be obliged to receive more than forty shillings in a single payment. Similarly, bronze coin is a legal tender only up to the amount of one shilling in all.

81. **What is a Pound Sterling?** In England people are continually paying and receiving money in pounds, but few could say exactly what a pound sterling means. No doubt it is represented by a coin called a sovereign, but what is a sovereign? Strictly speaking, **a sovereign is a piece of gold coined, in accordance with an Act of Parliament, at a British mint, still bearing the proper stamp of that mint, and weighing not less than $122\frac{1}{2}$ grains.** On the average the sovereigns issued from the mint ought to weigh 123·274 grains, but it is impossible to make each coin of that exact weight, and if this were done, the coins would soon be lessened in weight by wear. A sovereign is legal tender for a pound as long as it weighs $122\frac{1}{2}$ grains or more, and is not defaced; but, in reality, people are in the habit of paying and receiving sovereigns which are several grains less in weight than the law requires.

Twenty silver shillings are by law to be received as equal in value to a pound. This is necessary, in order that we may be able to pay a fraction of a pound, for a coin made of gold equal to the twentieth part of a pound would easily be lost, worn, or even blown away. But the silver in twenty shillings is not equal in value to the gold in a pound; its value varies with the gold price of silver, and, at present, twenty shillings are only worth about sixteen gold shillings and eight-pence, that is, $\frac{5}{6}$ of a pound. It is necessary to make the silver coin thus of less value than it is taken for, in order to render it unprofitable to melt the coin. In the same way, the metal in a bronze penny is worth only about the sixth part of a penny, so that people would lose a great deal by melting up or destroying pence.

82. **Paper Currency.** Instead of using actual coins of gold, silver, or bronze, it is common to make use of paper notes containing promises to pay money. When the sum of money to be paid is large, a bank note is much more convenient, being of far less weight than the coins, and less likely to be stolen. A five-pound bank note is a promise to pay five pounds to any person who has the note in his possession, and who asks for five pounds in exchange for the note at the office of the bank issuing the note. A **convertible bank note** is one which actually can be thus changed into the coins whenever it is desired, and so long as this is really the case, it is evident that the note is just as valuable as the coins, and is more convenient. The only fear is that, if a banker be allowed to issue these bank notes, he will not always have coins enough to pay them when presented. Very frequently banks have been obliged to stop payment; that is, to refuse to perform their promises. Nevertheless, when there is no other currency to be had, the bank notes often go on circulating like money. They are then called **inconvertible notes**, and there is said to be a **paper money.** A person is willing to receive paper currency in exchange for goods, if he believes that other people will take it from him again. But such paper currency is very bad, because its value will rise or fall according to the quantity issued, and people who owe money will often be able to pay their debts with less value than they received. The subject of bank notes and paper money, however, is too difficult for us to pursue in this Primer.

CHAPTER XIII.

CREDIT AND BANKING.

83. What Credit means. It is very important for those who would learn political economy to understand exactly what is meant by **credit.** John is said to give credit to Thomas when John leaves some of his property in the use of Thomas, expecting to have it returned at a future time. In short, any one who lends a thing **gives credit,** and he who borrows it **receives credit.** The word **credit** means **belief,** and John believes that he will get back his property from Thomas, though this, unfortunately, does not always prove to be the case. John is called the **creditor,** and Thomas the **debtor.**

It is not common, indeed, to speak of credit in the case of most articles : when a man borrows a horse, a book, a house, an engine, or other common article, and pays for its use, he is said to **hire** it, and what he pays for the use is called the hire, fare, or rent. In some countries, where coins are not yet used, people lend and borrow corn, oil, wine, rice, or any common commodity which all like to possess. In the parts of Africa where palm oil is produced in great quantities, people give and take credit in oil. But in all civilised countries it has become the practice to borrow and lend money. If a man needs an engine, and has nothing to buy it with, he goes and borrows money enough from the person who will lend it on the lowest terms, and then he buys the engine where he can get it most cheaply. Frequently, indeed, the man who sells the engine will give credit for its price, that is, will lend the sum of money to the buyer, just sufficient to enable him to buy it.

Credit is a very important thing, because, when properly employed, **it enables property to be put into the hands of those who will make the best use of it.** Many people have property but are unable to go into business, as is the case with women, children, old men, invalids, &c. Rich people perhaps have so much property that they do not care to trouble themselves with business, if they can get others to take the trouble for them. Even those who are engaged in business often have sums of money which they do not immediately want to use, and which they are willing to lend for a short time. On the other hand, there are many clever active men, who could do a great deal of work in establishing manufactories, sinking mines, or trading in goods, if they only had enough money to enable them to buy the requisite materials, tools, buildings, land, &c. A man must have some property of his own before he can expect to get credit; but with some property to fall back upon in case of need, and with a good character for honesty and ability, a trader can by credit obtain other people's capital to deal with.

84. **Loans on Mortgage.** Credit is given in many different ways; sometimes a man is assisted by a permanent loan from a relative or friend who has confidence in him. Enormous sums of money are lent, as it is called, upon **mortgage.** A man, for instance, who has built a cotton mill with· his own money, pledges the mill as security for a loan, that is, he gives his creditor a right to sell the mill unless the debt is paid when required. **The mill is called a mortgage or dead pledge,** because it becomes dead to the former owner, if he breaks the conditions of the loan. There are many institutions, such as insurance companies, building societies, &c., which have a great deal of capital to lend on mortgage, and many rich people invest their money in the same way. Thus a very large part of the houses, land, factories, shops, &c., are not really owned by the people who seem to own them, but by **mortgagees,** who have lent money on them.

Generally speaking, the interest paid for such loans is 4½ or 5 per cent. per annum, when the security is quite good, that is, when the property mortgaged is sure to sell for more than is lent upon it.   A considerable margin is always left to cover mistakes or alterations as regards the value of the property ; thus, if a house be said to be worth £1000, it will usually be security only for a debt of £700 or £800.   When the security is not so good, because the ownership or the value of the property mortgaged is doubtful, the rate of interest charged will be higher, and may be six, seven, or more per cent.   The surplus covers the risk, that is, compensates the lender, for the chance of losing what he lends.   Mortgage loans are generally made upon fixed capital like houses, mills, ships, &c., which last a long time ; but sometimes stocks of goods, such as cotton, wine, corn, &c., are mortgaged as security for temporary loans.

85. **Banking.**   A large part of the credit given, in a civilised country, is given by bankers, who may be said **to deal in credit,** or which comes to the same thing, **in debt.**   A banker usually carries on three or four different kinds of work, but his proper work is that of borrowing from persons who have ready money to lend, and lending it to those who want to buy goods.   As a shopkeeper sells his stock of goods, he receives money for it.   And, until he buys a new stock, he has no immediate need of this money.   Those, again, who receive salaries, dividends, rents, or other payments once a quarter, do not usually want to spend the whole at once.   Instead of keeping such money in a house, where it pays no interest and is liable to be stolen, lost, or burnt, it is much better to deposit it with a banker, that is, to lend it to a banker who will undertake to pay it back when it is wanted.   Generally speaking a merchant, manufacturer, or tradesman sends to his banker every day the money which he has received, and only keeps a few pounds to give change or make petty payments.   The advantages of thus depositing money with the banker are chiefly as follows :—

(1.) The money is safe, as the banker provides strong rooms, locked and guarded at night.

(2.) It is easy to pay the money away by means of cheques or written orders entitling the persons named therein to demand a specified sum of money from the banker.

(3.) The banker usually allows some interest for the money in his care.

Bankers receive deposits on various terms; sometimes the depositor engages to give seven days' notice before withdrawing his deposit; in other cases the money is lent to the banker for one, three, or six months certain, and the longer the time for which it is lent the better the rate of interest the banker can usually give. But a great deal of money is deposited **on current account**, that is, the customer puts his money into the bank, and draws it out just when he likes, without notice. In this case the banker gives very little interest, or none at all, because he has to keep much of the money ready for his customers, not knowing when it will be wanted.

Nevertheless, while some depositors are drawing their money out, others will be putting more in, and it is exceedingly unlikely that all the thousands of customers of a large bank will want their deposits at the same time. Thus it happens that the banker, in addition to his own capital, has a large stock of money always on hand, and he makes profit by lending out this money to other customers, who need credit.

There are various ways in which a banker arranges his loans; sometimes he lends upon the mortgage of goods, houses, and other property, or of shares in railways and government funds, in the way described; but this is not a proper way for a banker to employ much of his funds, because he may not be able to get back such loans rapidly enough when he needs them. One of the simplest ways of lending money is to allow customers to overdraw their accounts, that is, to draw more money out of the bank than they have put in.

But a banker naturally takes care not to allow over-drafts unless he has great confidence in his customer, or has received a guarantee of repayment from him or his friends.

86. Discount of Bills. The most common and proper way in which a banker gives credit and employs his funds is in the discount of bills, that is, in advancing money in exchange for a definite promise to pay it back at a stated time. Suppose that John Smith has sold a thousand pounds worth of cotton goods to Thomas Jones, a shopkeeper; several months will pass perhaps before Jones can sell the goods over the counter, and if he has not much capital, he agrees that John Smith shall give credit for the thousand pounds, but in the mean time draw a bill upon Jones. This bill would very likely be somewhat in this form—

LONDON, 1st February, 1878.

£1000, 0s. 0d.

      Three months after date pay to me or my order the sum of one thousand pounds, value received.

JOHN SMITH.

To Mr. Thomas Jones.

John Smith is said to be the **drawer** of the bill; Thomas Jones is the **drawee,** and the bill amounts to a claim on the part of John Smith that Thomas Jones owes him the sum named. If the drawee acknowledges that this is the case, he signifies it when the bill is presented to him, by writing on the back the word " accepted," together with his name.

Now if the drawer and drawee of a bill are persons of good credit, a banker will readily discount such a bill, that is, buy it up for the sum due, after subtracting interest at the rate of say five per cent. per annum for the length of time the bill has to run. The bill forms good security, because, when accepted, John Smith is bound to pay the thousand pounds when due, and if he fails, the drawee is liable. Such bills are often bought by one person after another, being **endorsed** by each to the next, that is, impressed with an order that the money shall be paid to the next person, named. When due the last owner must claim the money from John Smith, and if he refuses to pay, each owner has a claim upon the previous owners.

CHAPTER XIV.

CREDIT CYCLES.

87. Industry is Periodic. Everybody ought to understand that trade varies in activity, from time to time, in a periodic manner. **A thing is said to vary periodically, when it comes and goes at nearly equal intervals** like the sun, or rises and falls like the tides. Now, in industry, as Mr. William Langton pointed out twenty years ago, there are tides almost as regular as those of the sea. Shakespeare says truly—

> "There is a tide in the affairs of men,
> Which, taken at the flood, leads on to fortune."

Some of these tides depend upon the seasons of the year; business is more active in the spring and summer, and falls off in winter. It is comparatively easy to borrow money in January, February, March, June, July, August, and September; October and November are particularly bad months; the rate of interest then often runs up rapidly, and the bankruptcies in these months are more numerous than at any other time of year. April and May are also dangerous months, but in a less degree. Men of business should always bear these facts in mind, and, by being prepared beforehand, they may escape disaster.

There is also a much longer kind of tide in business, which usually takes somewhere about ten years to rise and fall. The cause of this tide is not well understood, but there can be no doubt that in some years men become confident and hopeful. They think that the country is going to be very prosperous, and that if they invest their capital in new factories, banks, railways, ships, or other enterprises, they will make much profit. When some people are thus hopeful, others readily become so too, just as a few cheerful people in a party make everybody cheerful. Thus the hopefulness gradually spreads itself through all the trades of the country. Clever men then propose schemes for new inventions and novel undertakings, and they find that they can readily get capitalists to subscribe for shares. This encourages other speculators to put forth proposals, and when the shares of some companies have risen in value, it is supposed that other shares will do so likewise. The most absurd schemes find supporters in a time of great hopefulness, and there thus arises what is called a bubble or mania.

88. **Commercial Bubbles or Manias.** When the schemes started during a bubble begin to be carried out, great quantities of materials are required for building, and the prices of these materials rise rapidly. The workpeople who produce these materials then earn high wages, and they spend these wages in better living, in pleasure, or in buying an unusual quantity of new clothes, furniture, &c. Thus the demand for commodities increases, and tradespeople make large profits. Even when there is no sufficient reason, the prices of the remaining commodities usually rise, as it is called, **by sympathy**, because those who deal in them think their goods will probably rise like other goods, and they buy up stocks in the hope of making profits. Every trader now wants to buy, because he believes that prices will rise higher and higher, and that, by selling at the right time, the loss of any subsequent fall of prices will be thrown upon other people.

This state of things, however. cannot go on very

long.   Those who have subscribed for shares in new companies have to pay up the calls, that is, find the capital which they promised.   They are obliged to draw out the money which they had formerly deposited in banks, and then the bankers have less to lend.   Manufacturers, merchants, and speculators, who are making or buying large stocks of goods, wish to borrow more and more money, in order that they may have a larger business, the profit seeming likely to be so great.   Then according to the laws of supply and demand, the price of money rises, which means that the rate of interest for short loans, from a week to three or six months in duration, is increased.   The bubble goes on growing, until the more venturesome and unscrupulous speculators have borrowed many times as much money as they themselves really possess.   **Credit is said to be greatly extended,** and a firm, which perhaps owns a capital worth ten thousand pounds, will have undertaken to pay two or three hundred thousand pounds, for the goods which they have bought on speculation.

But the sudden rise which, sooner or later, occurs in the rate of interest, is very disastrous to such speculators ; when they began to speculate interest was, perhaps, only two or three per cent. ; but when it becomes seven or eight per cent., there is fear that much of the profit will go in interest paid to the lenders of capital.   Moreover, those who lent the money, by discounting the speculators' bills, or making advances on the security of goods, become anxious to have it paid back.   Thus the speculators are forced at last to begin selling their stocks, at the best prices they can get.   As soon as some people begin to sell in this way, others who hold goods think they had better sell before the prices fall seriously ; then there arises a sudden rush to sell, and buyers being alarmed, refuse to buy except at much reduced rates.   The bad speculators now find themselves unable to maintain their credit, because, if they sell their large stocks at a considerable loss, their own real capital will be quite insufficient to cover this loss.   They are thus unable to pay what they have engaged to pay, and **stop payment**, or, in other words, become bankrupt.   This is very awkward for other people, manufacturers, for instance, who had sold goods to the bankrupts on credit ; they do not receive the money they expected, and as they also perhaps have borrowed money while making the goods, they become bankrupt likewise.   Thus the **discredit** spreads, and firms even which had borrowed only moderate sums of money, in proportion to their capital, are in danger of failing.

89. **Commercial Crisis or Collapse.** The state of things described in the last section is called a commercial collapse, because there is **a sudden falling in of prices, credit, and enterprise.**   It is also called **a Crisis, that is, a dangerous and decisive moment** (Greek, κρίνω, *to decide*), when it will soon be seen who is to become bankrupt, and who not.   No sooner has such a crisis arrived, than everything changes.   No one ventures to propose a new scheme, or a new company, because he knows that people in general have great difficulty in paying up what they promised to the schemes started during the bubble.   **This bubble is now burst,** and it is found that many of the new works and undertakings from which people expected so much profit, are absurd and hopeless mistakes.   It was proposed to make railways where there was nothing to carry ; to sink mines where there was no coal nor metal ; to build ships which would not sail ; all kinds of impracticable schemes have to be given up, and the capital spent upon them is lost.

Not only does this collapse ruin many of the subscribers to these schemes, but it presently causes workpeople to be thrown out of employment.   The more successful schemes indeed are carried out, and, for a year or two, give employment to builders, iron-manufacturers, and others, who furnish the materials.

But as these schemes are completed by degrees, no one ventures to propose new ones ; people have been frightened by the losses and bankruptcies and frauds brought to light in the collapse, and when some people are afraid, others readily become frightened likewise by sympathy. In matters of this kind men of business are much like a flock of sheep which follow each other without any clear idea why they do so. In a year or two the prices of iron, coal, timber, &c., are reduced to the lowest point ; great losses are suffered by those who make or deal in such materials, and many workmen are out of employment. The working classes then have less to spend on luxuries, and the demand for other goods decreases ; trade in general becomes depressed ; many people find themselves paupers, or spend their savings accumulated during previous years. Such a **state of depression** may continue for two or three years, until speculators have begun to forget their failures, or a new set of younger men, unacquainted with disaster, think they see a way to make profits. During such a period of depression, too, the richer people who have more income than they spend, save it up in the banks. Business men as they sell off their stocks of goods leave the money received in the banks ; thus by degrees capital becomes abundant, and the rate of interest falls. After a time bankers, who were so very cautious at the time of the collapse, find it necessary to lend their increasing funds, and credit is improved. Then begins a new credit cycle, which probably goes through much the same course as the previous one.

90. **Commercial Crises are Periodic.** It would be a very useful thing if we were able to foretell when a bubble or a crisis was coming, but it is evidently impossible to predict such matters with certainty. All kinds of events—wars, revolutions, new discoveries, treaties of commerce, bad or good harvests, &c.—may occur to decrease or increase the activity of trade.

Nevertheless, **it is wonderful how often a great commercial crisis has happened about ten years after the previous one.** During the last century, when trade was so different from what it now is, there were crises in or near the years 1753, 1763, 1772 or '3, 1783, and 1793. In this century there have been crises in the years 1815, 1825, 1836-9, 1847, 1857, 1866, and there would probably have been a crisis in 1876 or 1877 had it not been for an exceptional collapse in America in 1873. There is at present (February, 1878) the great depression of trade which marks the completion of one cycle and the commencement of a new one.

Good vintage years on the continent of Europe, and droughts in India, recur every ten or eleven years, and it seems probable that commercial crises are connected with a periodic variation of weather, affecting all parts of the earth, and probably arising from increased waves of heat received from the sun at average intervals of ten years and a fraction. A greater supply of heat increases the harvests, makes capital more abundant and trade more successful, and thus helps to create the hopefulness out of which a bubble arises. A falling off in the sun's heat makes bad harvests and deranges many enterprises in different parts of the world. This is likely to break the bubble and bring on a commercial collapse.

Generally, **a credit cycle,** as Mr. John Mills of Manchester has called it, will last **about ten years.** The first three years will witness depressed trade, with want of employment, falling prices, low rate of interest, and much poverty; then there will be perhaps three years of active, healthy trade, with moderately-rising prices, a reasonable rate of interest, fair employment, and improving credit; then come some years of unduly-excited trade, turning into a bubble or mania, and ending in a collapse, as already described. This collapse will occupy the last of the ten years, so that the whole credit cycle will, on the average, be as follows:—

YEARS.									
I	2	3	4	5	6	7	8	9	10
DEPRESSED· TRADE.			HEALTHY TRADE.			EXCITED TRADE.		*Bubble.*	*Collapse.*

It is not to be supposed that things go as regularly as is here stated; sometimes the cycle lasts only nine, or even eight years, instead of ten; minor bubbles and crises sometimes happen in the course of the cycle, and disturb its regularity. Nevertheless, it is wonderful how often the great collapse comes at the end of the cycle, in spite of war or peace, or other interfering causes.

91. **How to avoid Loss by Crises.** Now, these bubbles and crises are very disastrous things; they lead to the ruin of many people, and there are few old families who have not lost money at one collapse or another. The working-classes are often much injured; many are thrown out of employment, and others, not seeing why their wages should be reduced, make things worse by strikes, which, after a collapse, cannot possibly succeed. It is most important, therefore, that all people—working-people, capitalists, speculators, and all connected with any kind of business— should remember that **very prosperous trade is sure to be followed by a collapse and by bad trade.** When, therefore, things look particularly promising, investors should be unusually careful into what undertakings they put their money. **As a general rule, it is foolish to do just what other people are doing, because there are almost sure to be too many people doing the same thing.** If, for instance, the price of coal rises high, and coal-owners make large profits, there

are certain to be many people sinking new mines. Such a time is just the worst one for buying shares in a coal-mine, because, in the course of a few years, there will be a multitude of new mines opened, the next collapse of trade will decrease the demand for coal, and then there will be great losses in the coal business.   This is what has happened in the last few years in England, and the same thing has happened over and over again in other trades, As a general rule, **the best time to begin a new factory, mine, or business of any kind, is when the trade is depressed, and when wages and interest are low.**   Mining, building, or other work can then be done more cheaply than at other times, and the new works will be ready to start just when business is becoming active and there are few other new works opening.

This rule, indeed, does not apply to the schemers, speculators, or **promoters,** as they are called, who start so many companies.   These people make it their business to have new schemes and shares to offer just when people are in a mind to buy, that is, during a bubble or time of excited trade.   They take care to sell their own shares before the collapse comes, and it is their dupes who bear all the loss.   A prudent man, therefore, would never invest in any new thing during a mania or bubble ; on the contrary, he would sell all property of a doubtful or speculative value, when its price is high, and invest it in the very best shares or government funds, of which the value cannot fall much during the coming collapse.   The wisest men have been deluded during manias; and in the Library of the Royal Society is shown a letter from Sir Isaac Newton requesting a friend to buy shares for him in the South Sea Company, just at the moment when the South Sea Bubble was at its worst.   Let people take warning by Sir Isaac Newton, and never speculate in a thing because other people are doing the same ; then these bubbles and collapses will be prevented, or will become much less disastrous. Credit cycles will go on until the public learn to look out for them, and act accordingly. Business men must become bold during depressed trade, careful during excited trade, instead of acting exactly in the opposite way. It is only a knowledge of these credit cycles which can prevent them, and this is the reason why I have said so much about them in this Primer.

CHAPTER XV.

THE FUNCTIONS OF GOVERNMENT.

92. Functions mean performances (Latin, *fungi*, *functus*, to perform), and the functions of government mean those things which a government ought to do, —the duties which it undertakes to perform, or the services which it may be expected to render to the people governed. These functions are commonly divided into two classes—

　(1) The necessary functions.
　(2) The optional functions.

The **necessary functions** of a government are such as it is obliged to undertake; thus it must defend the nation against foreign enemies, it must keep the peace within the country, and prevent insurrections which might threaten the existence of the government itself; it must also punish evildoers who break the laws, and try to become rich by robbery; it must also maintain law courts in which the disputes of its subjects can be fairly decided, and set at rest. These are far from being all the necessary functions.

The **optional functions** of government consist of those kinds of work which a government can execute with advantage, such as providing a good currency, establishing a uniform system of weights and measures, constructing and maintaining the roads, carrying letters through a national post office, keeping up a national observatory and a meteorological office,

&c. The optional functions are in fact very numerous, and there is hardly any end to the things which one government or another has provided for the people. It would be a most important work, if it were possible, to decide exactly what undertakings a government ✓ should take upon itself, and what it should leave to the free action of other people ; but it is impossible to lay down any precise rules upon this subject. The characters and habits and circumstances of nations differ so much, that what is good in one case might be bad in another. Thus in Russia the government makes all the railways, and the same is the case in the Australian States ; but it does not at all follow that, because this is necessary or desirable in those countries, therefore it is desirable in England, or Ireland, or the United States. Experience shows that though the English Post Office is very profitable, the Postal Telegraphs cannot at present be made to pay. There can be no doubt that it **would be altogether ruinous to put the enormous system of English railways under the management of government officers.** Each case has thus to be judged upon its own merits, and all that the political economist can do is to point out the general advantages and disadvantages of government management.

93. **The Advantage of Government Management.** There is often immense economy in having a single establishment to do a certain kind of work for the whole country. For instance, a weather office in London can get daily telegraphic reports of the weather in all parts of the kingdom and many parts of Europe; combining and comparing these reports it can form a much better opinion about the coming weather than would be possible to private persons, and this opinion can be rapidly made known by the telegraph and newspapers. The few thousand pounds spent by the government yearly on the meteorological office are inconsiderable compared with the services

which it may render to the public by preventing ship-wrecks, colliery explosions, and other great disasters and inconveniences which often arise from our ignorance of the coming weather. It is certainly proper then to make meteorological observation one of the functions of government.

Great economy would arise, again, if an establishment like the post-office were created in Great Britain in order to convey small goods and parcels. At present there are a great number of parcel companies, but they often send a cart a long way to deliver a single parcel. In London some half a dozen independent companies send carts all over the immense town; each of the chief railway companies has its own system of delivering parcels, and the larger shops have their own delivery vans as well. Thus there is an enormous loss of horse power and men's time. If a government postal system undertook the work, only one cart would deliver goods in each street, and as there might be a parcel for almost every house, or sometimes several, there would be an almost incredible saving in the distance travelled and the time taken up. This illustrates the economy which may arise from government management.

94. **The Disadvantage of Government Management.** On the other hand there is great evil in the government undertaking any work which can be fairly done by private persons or companies. Officers of the government are seldom dismissed when once employed, or, if turned away, they receive pensions. Thus when the government establishes any new work, it cannot stop it without great expense, and the work is usually carried on whether it is done economically or not. Then again, government officers, knowing that they will not be dismissed without a pension, are commonly less active and careful than men in private employment. For the work which they do they are paid at a higher rate than in private establishments.

It is therefore very undesirable that the Government

should take any kind of work into its own hands, unless it is perfectly clear that the work will be done much better, and more cheaply than private persons could do it. There is a balance of advantages and disadvantages to be considered : the advantage of a single great establishment with plenty of funds; and the disadvantage that work is always done more expensively by Government. In the case of the post-office, the advantages greatly outweigh the disadvantages; the same would probably be the case with a well-arranged parcel post; in the postal telegraphs, there are many advantages, but they are obtained at a considerable loss of revenue. If the state were to buy up and manage the railways of Great Britain, the advantages would be comparatively small, but the losses would be enormous. In America the express or parcel companies are so admirably managed that they do the work more safely and better than the Government post office. There can be little doubt, too, that the American railways and telegraphs are far better managed now than they would be if acquired by the Federal Government.

CHAPTER XVI.

TAXATION.

95. **There must be Taxes.** Whether governments undertake more or less functions, it is certain that we must have some kind of government, and that this government will spend a great deal of money. This money, too, can very seldom be obtained in the form of real profit on the work done, so that it must be raised by taxation. We generally apply the name tax to any payment required from individuals towards the expenses of the local or general government. We may easily indeed be taxed without being aware of it ; thus, nearly the half of every penny paid for posting a letter

is a tax, and a town may be taxed through the price of gas or water.

At one time or another, and in one country or another, taxes have been raised in every imaginable way. The **Poll Tax** was a payment required from every **poll** or head of the population, man, woman, or child. This was considered a very grievous tax and has never been levied in England since the reign of William III. The **Hearth Tax** consisted of a payment for each hearth in a house; then a rich family with a large house and many hearths paid far more than a poor family with only one or two hearths. But as people did not like the taxgatherer coming into the house to count the hearths, the window tax was substituted, because the tax-gatherer could walk round the outside of the house, and count the windows. Now, in England, we do not tax the light of heaven at all, but we fix a man's payments by the rent of his house, the amount of his income, or the quantity of wine and beer he drinks.

96. **Direct and Indirect Taxes.** Taxes are called **direct taxes** when the payment is made by the person who is intended to bear the sacrifice. This is the case generally with the assessed taxes, or the charges made upon people who have menservants, private carriages, &c. As most people keep carriages only for their own comfort, they cannot make other people repay the cost of the tax. But if a carrier or tradesman were taxed for his carts, he would be sure to make his customers repay it; thus the tax would not be direct, and carriages employed in trade are therefore exempt from taxation. Other taxes in England, which are generally direct ones, are the income-tax, the dog-tax, the poor-rates, the house-duty; but a tax which is usually direct, may sometimes become indirect, and it is often impossible to say what is really **the incidence of a tax**, that is, the manner in which it falls upon different classes of the population.

Indirect taxes are paid in the first place by

merchants and tradesmen, but it is understood that they recover the amount paid from their customers. The principal part of such taxes in England consist of the **customs duties** levied upon wine, spirits, tobacco, and a few other articles, when they are imported for use in this country. **Excise duties** are similar duties levied upon like goods produced within the kingdom. These were called **excise,** because it was originally the practice actually to cut off a portion of the goods themselves, and take it as the duty. In England, excise duties are now levied on a few things only, such as spirits and beer; and care is taken to make the excise duty as nearly as possible equal to the customs duty on the same kind of imported goods. English brandy pays a duty equivalent to that on French brandy, and the matter is arranged so that the duty shall neither encourage nor discourage the making of English brandy. Thus the trade is left as free as it can be, consistently with raising a large revenue. Another important class of indirect taxes consist of **the stamp duties,** which are payments required from people when they make legal agreements of various kinds. According to law, deeds, leases, cheques, receipts, contracts, and many other documents are not legally valid unless they be stamped, and the cost of the stamp varies from a penny up to hundreds or even thousands of pounds, according to the value of the property dealt with. Stamp duties are probably in most cases indirect taxes, but it would be very difficult to say who really bears the cost; this must depend much upon circumstances.

97. **Maxims of Taxation.** Adam Smith first stated certain rules. or maxims, which should guide the statesman in laying on taxes; they are such good rules that everybody who studies political economy ought to learn them. They are as follows—

(1) The subjects of every state ought to contribute towards the support of the government, as nearly as possible, in proportion to their respective abilities; that

is, in proportion to the revenue which they respectively enjoy under the protection of the state.

This we may call the **maxim of equality**, and equality consists in everybody paying, in one way or another, about an equal percentage of the wages, salary, or other income which he receives. In England the taxes amount to something like ten per cent., or one pound in every ten pounds, and this is pretty equally borne by different classes of society. It is probable, however, that the very rich do not pay as much as they ought to do. At the same time those who are too poor to pay income tax, and who do not drink nor smoke, are almost entirely free from taxation in this country; they pay very little, except poor rates. It would be impossible to invent any one tax which could be equally levied upon all persons. The income tax is a tax of so many pence in every pound of a person's income, but it is impossible to make people state their income exactly, and poor people could never be got to pay such a tax. Hence it is necessary to put on a certain number of different taxes so that those who manage to escape one tax shall be made to pay in some other way.

(2) The tax which each individual is bound to pay ought to be certain, and not arbitrary. The time of payment, the manner of payment, the quantity to be paid, ought all to be clear and plain. This is the **maxim of certainty**, and it is very important, because, if a tax is not certainly known, the tax-gatherers can oppress people, requiring more or less as they choose. In this case it is very probable that they will become corrupt, and will receive bribes to induce them to lower the tax. On this account duties ought never to be levied according to the value of goods, or *ad valorem*, as it is said. Wine, for instance, varies in value immensely according to its quality and reputation, but it is impossible for the custom-house officer to say exactly what this value is. If he takes the statement of the people who import the wine, they

will be tempted to tell lies, and say that the value is less than it really is. And as it would not be easy to prove the guilt either of the customs officer or of the importers, it is to be feared that some officers will receive bribes. But if the wine is taxed simply according to its quantity, the amount of duty is known with great certainty, and fraud can easily be detected. The same remarks apply more or less to every kind of goods which varies much in quality.

(3) Every tax ought to be levied at the time, and in the manner, in which it is most likely to be convenient for the contributor to pay it. This is **the maxim of convenience,** and the reason for it is sufficiently obvious. As government only exists for the good of the people at large, of course it ought to give the people as little trouble as possible. And as the Government has immensely more money at its command than any private person, it ought to arrange so as to demand a tax when the taxpayer is likely to be able to pay it. Thus there seems to be no sufficient reason why the government should make people pay the income-tax in January, when they are likely to have plenty of other bills to pay. In respect of this maxim, the customs and excise duties are very good taxes, because a person pays duty whenever he buys a bottle of spirits or an ounce of tobacco. If he does not want to pay taxes, let him leave off drinking and smoking, which will probably be better for him in every way. At any rate, if he can afford to drink spirits and smoke tobacco, he can afford something for the expenses of government. The penny receipt duty, again, is in this respect a good tax, because when a person is receiving money he is sure to be able to spare one penny for the State, and he is generally so glad to get his money that he thinks nothing of the penny.

(4) Every tax ought to be so contrived as both to take out and to keep out of the pockets of the people as little as possible over and above what it brings

into the public treasury. This is the **maxim of economy**. Thus, a tax ought not to be imposed if it would require a great many officers to collect it, and thus waste much of what is collected, or if it disturbs trade and makes things dearer than they would otherwise be. Again, the government ought not to cause people to lose time and money in paying the taxes, because this is just as bad for them as if they paid so much more taxes. In this respect the stamp-duties are very bad taxes, because in many cases it is requisite for a person to take his deeds and other documents to the stamp-office and lose his time, or else employ lawyers and agents to do it for him, who charge considerable fees. So troublesome are some of the stamp-duties that in many cases people neglect to have their agreements stamped, and prefer to trust to the honesty of those they deal with. Such agreements are thus often rendered of no legal value, and the government, for the sake of sixpence or a shilling, practically denies law to the people.

98. **Protection and Free Trade.** Almost every government has employed taxation at one time or another, for the purpose of encouraging industry within the country. It is often supposed that if purchasers are prevented from buying foreign goods, they will have to buy home-made goods, and thus manufacturers at home will be kept busy, and there will be plenty of employment. This is altogether a fallacy, which we may call the **fallacy of Protection**, but it is one which readily takes hold of people's minds. No tradesman or manufacturer likes to see himself underbid by those who offer better goods at lower prices. When foreign goods, then, are preferred by purchasers, the home manufacturers of such goods complain bitterly, and join together to persuade people that they are being injured by foreign trade. There is still so much national pride and animosity, that a nation does not like to be told that it is being beaten by foreigners.

The manufacturers, misled by their own self-interest, use all kinds of bad arguments to show that if foreign products were kept out of the country, they could make as good ones in a little time, and then they could employ many people, and add to the wealth of the country. They fall, in fact, into **the fallacy of making work** before described (section 55), and argue as if the purpose of work was to work, and not to enjoy abundant supplies of the necessaries and comforts of life.

Now it is impossible to deny that certain owners of lands and mines and works may be benefited by putting duties upon foreign goods of the kind which they want to produce. Those who are already enjoying the advantage of such improper duties may, of course, be injured when they are removed. But what we have in political economy to look to, is not the selfish interests of any particular class of people, but the good of the whole population. Protectionists overlook two facts—(1) that the object of industry is to make goods abundant and cheap; (2) that it is impossible to import cheap foreign goods without exporting home-made goods of some sort to pay for them.

We have already learnt the obvious truth that wealth is to be increased by producing it in the place most suitable for its production. Now the only sure proof that a place is suitable is the fact that the commodities there produced are cheap and good. If foreign manufacturers can underbid home-producers, this is the best, and in fact the only conclusive proof that the things can be made more cheaply and successfully abroad. But then it may be objected, what is to become of workmen at home, if all our supplies be got from another country. The reply is, that such a state of things could not exist. Foreigners would never think of sending us goods unless we paid for them, either in other goods, or in money. Now, if we pay in goods, workmen will of course be needed to make those goods; and the more we buy from abroad, the more we shall need of home produce to send in exchange. Thus, the purchase of foreign goods encourages home manufactures in the best possible way, because it encourages just those branches of industry for which the country is most suited, and by which wealth is most abundantly created.

99. **The Mercantile Theory.** Perhaps, however, it will be objected that our foreign imports will be paid for not in goods but in money; thus the country will be gradually drained of its wealth. This is **the old fallacy of the Mercantile Theory,** which was to the effect that a country becomes rich by bringing gold and silver into it. It is an absurd fallacy, because we can get no benefit by accumulating stocks of gold and silver. In fact, to keep precious metals causes a loss of interest upon their value; people who are rich may afford to have costly plate, and the pleasures they derive from it may be worth the interest. But to have more gold, or silver money than is just sufficient to make the ordinary payments of trade causes dead loss of interest. Nor is there any fear that the country will be drained of money entirely. For, if money became scarce, its value would rise according to the laws of supply and demand, and prices of goods would fall; then imports would decrease, and exports increase. It is only a country like Australia or North America, possessing gold or silver mines, which could go on paying money for its imports, and then it is quite right it should do so, the metal being a commodity which can be cheaply produced in the country. Gold and silver must be got out of mines, and therefore a country which buys goods with money must either have such mines, or else get the metal from other countries which possess mines. In no case, then, can we import foreign commodities without producing at home goods of equivalent value to pay for them, and thus we see beyond all doubt that foreign trade is

a means of increasing, not decreasing, the activity of industry at home.

100. **Is Political Economy a Dismal Science?** This is only a Primer, a very brief and elementary account of some parts of political economy, and it is evidently impossible to argue out the subjects of such a science in so small a compass. But the purpose of this little treatise will be fulfilled if those who begin with the primer can be persuaded to go on and study larger works on the science. But even he who has read only thus far must know that political economy is no cold-blooded or dismal science, as people say. Is it a dismal thing to relieve the labourer of his load, or to spread his table with the most nutritious food? No doubt the science is dismal enough so far as it leads us to reflect upon the needless misery existing on every side. It is dismal to think of the hundreds of thousands who lengthen out a weary life in workhouses and prisons and infirmaries. Strikes are dismal; lock-outs are dismal; want of employment, bankruptcy, dear bread, famine, are all dismal things. But is it political economy which causes them? **Is not our science more truly described as that beneficent one, which, if sufficiently studied, would banish such dismal things, by teaching us to use our powers wisely in relieving the labours and misery of mankind.**

END.

www.ingramcontent.com/pod-product-compliance
Lightning Source LLC
Chambersburg PA
CBHW030612270326
41927CB00007B/1138